CONQUEST AND CRISIS
Studies in Joshua, Judges and Ruth

A Relief Map of Palestine, showing the deep rift of the Jordan Valley, culminating in the Dead Sea, about 1300 feet below sea level. Matson Photo Service

CONQUEST AND CRISIS
Studies in Joshua,
Judges and Ruth

by
John J. Davis

BAKER BOOK HOUSE
Grand Rapids, Michigan

Library of Congress Catalog Card Number: 70-88244

ISBN: 0-8010-2822-1

First printing, August 1969
Second printing, January 1973
Third printing, June 1974
Fourth printing, March 1976
Fifth printing, July 1977

Baker Book House Company and BMH — copublishers

PRINTED IN THE UNITED STATES OF AMERICA

To my beloved wife Carolyn
and our daughter Debbie

ACKNOWLEDGMENTS

The author wishes to express his deep gratitude to those who contributed valuable help in the preparation of this volume.

They are as follows:

Mrs. Irene Anderson who did an excellent job of typing the manuscripts.

Mr. Robert Ibach who prepared the chronological chart and maps.

Dr. John C. Whitcomb who made valuable suggestions regarding the content and literary style of this volume.

Dr. Benjamin Hamilton who prepared the index to the book.

CONTENTS

List of Illustrations

TRANSLITERATION

Whenever possible, Hebrew and Greek words have been transliterated according to the following form:

Greek	Consonants	Vocalization
α — a	א — '	— ā
ᾳ — a	ב — b, b̠	— a
ε — e	ג — g, g̠	— e
η — ē	ד — d, d̠	— ē
ο — o	ה — h	— ê
ω — ō	ו — w	— i
ζ — z	ז — z	— î
	ח — ḥ	
θ — th	ט — ṭ	— o
ξ — x	י — y	— û
υ — u	כ — k, k̠	— u
φ — ph	ל — l	— ( )e
χ — ch	מ — m	
ϥ — ps	נ — n	
' — h	ס — s	
	ע — '	
	פ — p, p̠	
	צ — ṣ	
	ק — q	
	ר — r	
	שׁ — ś	
	שׁ — š	
	ת — t, t̠	

PREFACE

In spite of the tremendous importance of the books of Joshua, Judges, and Ruth, little has appeared in recent years which deals with the texts of these books and their historical and cultural backgrounds. Unfortunately, much of that which has appeared in print has been oriented in two extreme directions. Liberal writers have consistently rewritten the history of the patriarchal and conquest periods. This approach minimizes the historical value of the books in question and relates much of the material to very late periods in Israel's history. On the other hand, some writers have obscured the texts through excessive spiritualization and typology. While this is supposed to have practical value, in the long run it makes the understanding of these books most difficult for the Bible student and layman. It is the view of this writer that if this era of Israel's history is to be properly understood, both these extremes should be avoided. This volume is designed to deal with the text of these books as viewed in the light of their historical, cultural, and theological backgrounds.

The writer is indebted to his students who have studied these books with him over the past few years. Their suggestions have been most helpful in developing a careful analysis of this period of Israel's history.

The basic aim of this volume is to introduce the student to the historical and theological developments of the conquest and settlement period by a careful study of the text of Joshua, Judges, and Ruth. While the volume deals primarily with the Biblical text and its interpretation, archaeological and historical data are brought into view on many points in order to help clarify difficult problems. Since extended quotations from the Biblical text do not appear in this volume for lack of space, it is desirable that the student study this volume with an open Bible.

FOREWORD

John C. Whitcomb, Jr., Th.D.

The books of Joshua and Judges constitute a vital message from the living God to His people in every age. Primarily, they tell of a God who is perfectly able to keep His covenant promises to Israel, even by means of stupendous miracles, and even though the fulfillment be delayed through many generations.

This same God is today preparing Israel for her final entrance into the Promised Land. Even as He prepared a highway "for Israel in the day that he came up out of the land of Egypt," so also "it shall come to pass in that day, that the Lord will set his hand again *the second time* to recover the remnant of his people, that shall remain . . . and will assemble the outcasts of Israel, and gather together the dispersed of Judah from the four corners of the earth" (Isa. 11:16, 11-12).

Thus, for the nation of Israel, the Book of Joshua is the foreshadowing of an even greater entrance into the Promised Land, at the end of this age. The major difference, of course, is that Joshua did not have the power of an endless life; and his death was followed by periods of great apostasy, during which "there was no king in Israel: every man did that which was right in his own eyes" (Judg. 21:25). The final Joshua, Israel's Messiah, will not die, but instead, "of the increase of his government and of peace there shall be no end" (Isa. 9:7).

Christians have found in Joshua and Judges a most remarkable parallel to the Book of Ephesians. Christ, our Joshua, has led us from the wilderness of sin and spiritual death into the land of fellowship and service with Him. But this land, like the Promised Land of Joshua's day, is filled to overflowing with the enemies of God. Joshua was commanded to "be strong and of good courage" and to meditate in God's Word day and night. Thus, "there shall not any man be able to stand before thee all the days of thy life" (Josh. 1:5-9). So now, we are admonished to "be strong in the Lord, and in the strength of his might. Put on the whole armor of God, that ye may be able to stand against the wiles of the devil" (Eph. 6:10-11). And as for

Joshua, so for us, the one great offensive weapon is "the sword of the Spirit, which is the Word of God" (v. 17). When Israel took her eyes off the Lord, she was invaded from every direction and utterly humiliated. Today, Christians who turn their eyes from Christ become as "children, tossed to and fro and carried about with every wind of doctrine, by the sleight of men, in craftiness, after the wiles of error" (Eph. 4:14).

Dr. John Davis, a faithful colleague on the faculty of Grace Theological Seminary, has done good service to the Church of our Lord Jesus Christ in preparing this study of Joshua, Judges and Ruth. Taking into consideration all the significant light that has been shed upon these inspired narratives from the science of archaeology, Dr. Davis has sought to focus our attention on the basic problems and lessons of these books. While his analysis is designed primarily for the layman, he has not hesitated to dig into the riches of the Hebrew text to explain important words that escape the attention of those who are at the mercy of translators. Thus, we have in this study a dependable introduction to a fascinating portion of God's Word. May we in our day, like Joshua in his, learn how to meditate in this infallible Book day and night, and thus have our way made prosperous and find good success in His service (Josh. 1:8).

JOSHUA

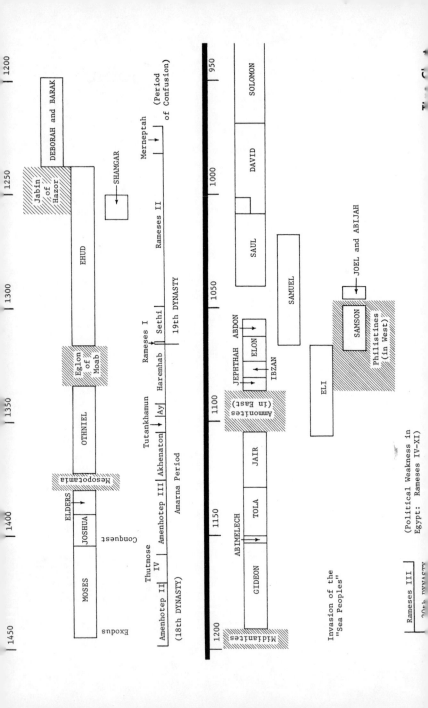

Chapter 1

INTRODUCTION

I. THE SURVIVAL OF A NATION

The record of Israel's exodus from the land of Egypt and preservation in the barren wilderness of Sinai constitutes one of the most captivating stories in the Bible. Equally thrilling are the accounts of Israel's conquest of the land of Canaan under the leadership of the man Joshua. The years spent in conquest and settlement were crucial ones in the history of Israel. A comprehensive record of these events is found in the first eight books of the Bible. The first five books, known as the Pentateuch, give us the history of the Hebrews *up to* their entrance into the land of Canaan, while the books of Joshua, Judges and Ruth continue that history by describing the conquest and settlement *in* the land of Canaan.

In this chapter we will examine the historical, cultural and religious setting for the conquest and settlement era as illuminated by recent archaeological and historical studies.

A. *Historical Setting*

1. *The Biblical Data*

When did the conquest of Canaan take place? This question must be considered before one attempts to describe the cultural setting for these events. At present there is an absence of agreement upon this question. Many scholars, refusing to accept the historical accuracy of the numbers of the Bible, date these events in the thirteenth century B.C.[1] Others, following the chronological data given in several key texts, date the conquest in the fourteenth century B.C. The latter view appears to be the preferable view in the light of Biblical evidence and Egyptian history. According to I Kings 6:1 the exodus from Egypt took place 480 years before the fourth year of Solomon. The date for the fourth year of Solomon is generally regarded as 966 B.C. This would mean that the exodus took

---

[1]Yohanan Aharoni, *The Land of the Bible*, Trans. A. F. Rainey (Philadelphia: The Westminster Press, 1962), p. 178 Note #10.

place about 1446/5 B.C. In order to arrive at the date for the beginning of the conquest under Joshua, one need only deduct the 40 years spent in the wilderness (Exod. 16:35, Num. 14:33 34). The campaigns of Joshua, therefore, began about 1405 B.C.[2] The Judge Jephthah places 300 years between Israel's sojourn at Heshbon and about the second year of his judgeship (Judg. 11:26). If we add 38 years to cover the period from the exodus to Heshbon and 144 years from Jephthah to the fourth year of Solomon, we find that the total number of years between the exodus and Solomon's fourth year is about 482.[3] This accords well with the information given in I Kings 6:1. The chronological setting for the events recorded in the Book of Joshua should be considered as the fourteenth century B.C. According to Caleb's statement in Joshua 14:10 the major battles recorded in Joshua 1:1–14:1 lasted for a period of about seven years.[4]

2. Egypt and Palestine

The information obtained by archaeological research and a careful study of the Biblical records indicate that the exodus should be placed in the middle of the fifteenth century B.C. (i.e., 1445 B.C.). This would mean that Joseph rose to power during the Twelfth Dynasty in Egypt, i.e., in the nineteenth century B.C. Exodus 1:8 informs us that a "new king" rose up against Egypt.[5] This undoubtedly refers to one of the Hyksos

---

[2]John Rea, "The Time of the Oppression and Exodus," *Grace Journal* (Winona Lake: Grace Theological Seminary, 1961), Vol. 2, No. 1.

――――――, "New Light on the Wilderness Journey and the Conquest, *Grace Journal*, Vol. 2, No. 2.

[3]The extra two years can probably be adjusted on the basis of overlapping judgeships during this period.

[4]According to Caleb's statement, 45 years had passed since the giving of the promise to him (Josh. 14:10). That promise was given to him 38 years before the crossing of the Jordan (cf. Num. 14:24). The major battles, therefore, took about seven years. Josephus (*Ant.* V: 1:19) gives the duration of the conquest as five years.

[5]The Hebrew expression translated "rose up over Egypt" is *wayāqām melek ḥādāš 'al miṣrāyim* and is better rendered "rose up *against* Egypt." Note the use of this expression elsewhere (Deut. 19:11, 28:7; Judg. 9:18, 20:5; II Sam. 18:31; II Kings 16:7).

kings who ruled in the Delta area. The Hyksos dominated lower Egypt for about 150 years and in the middle of the sixteenth century were driven out of Egypt. This brought about a revival of native Egyptian rule and the establishment of the Eighteenth Dynasty in the land. It is interesting to note that the Israelites were not driven out with the Hyksos even though they both lived in the Delta area. The Eighteenth Dynasty pharaohs continued to enslave the Israelites until the Lord raised up Moses to lead them out of the land in 1445 B.C. This great exodus probably took place during the reign of Amenhotep II (1450-1423 B.C.).[6] It is significant, indeed, that the Lord should deliver His people from Egypt when Egypt was enjoying unparalleled economic growth and political control over countries to the north. What better way could the Lord demonstrate His sovereign power over the nations of the world and prove conclusively that Israel was indeed His "son" and "firstborn" (cf. Exod. 4:22)?

When Israel was about to enter Canaan, another amazing turn of events took place. Egypt, which had unqualified control over Palestine, began to weaken under the leadership of Pharaoh Amenhotep III (1410-1372 B.C.). Throughout the latter years of his reign and during the reign of his son Akhenaten (1380-1363 B.C.) there was a decided decline in interest in Palestinian holdings and the result was that many of the petty kings of Palestine revolted from Egyptian rule. Other cities in Palestine were quite frustrated over the lack of defense provided by these pharaohs and in desperation wrote many letters to Amarna, the capital city of Akhenaten, pleading for help. These letters, written in cuneiform script, were discovered at Tell el-Amarna in Egypt in 1887 and are a valuable commentary on the political and military climate in Palestine and Syria during the conquest era. The letters constantly mention the need for military aid from Egypt in order to stop the invasions conducted by neighboring city-states and groups known as the "Habiru." It is possible that in some cases the "Habiru" invasions might be a reference to Israelite military activity, although recent studies

---

[6]For further discussion of this problem and its solution, see John Rea, *loc. cit.*

make it clear that the term "Habiru" is not to be equated with "Hebrew" as some have attempted to do.

From a purely human point of view it seems quite strange that a powerful nation such as Egypt would relinquish its iron grip on Palestine especially when it had the resources to maintain that control. But from a Biblical point of view it is quite evident that the Lord was again preparing the way for His people. This radical change in Egyptian foreign policy came just at the time Israel was about to enter Canaan. This meant that Israel would not have to face the mighty armies of Egypt in its conquest of the land, but only the local armies and military coalitions. You will notice that there is no mention of Egyptian resistence anywhere in the Biblical accounts of the conquest. Even when the Egyptians did enter Canaan during this period, it was only to march along the coast in order to contact their enemy to the north, the Hittites. One cannot but thrill at the marvelous way God undertakes for His people in the most difficult circumstances.

The conquest and settlement period has been greatly illuminated by recent archaeological discoveries in Palestine. The Late Bronze period (*ca.* 1500-1200 B.C.) is characterized by the destruction of many cities. This wide-spread series of destructions was due to a number of factors. First, it seems clear that as the Hyksos were driven out of Egypt they settled in certain Palestinian cities, and when the Egyptians observed this, they continued their pursuit of the Hyksos into Palestine destroying many of their strongholds. Secondly, following the expulsion of the Hyksos, the Egyptians showed renewed interest in Palestine under the Thutmoside rulers and this led to a number of campaigns aimed at bringing Palestinian city-states under Egyptian control again. Finally, the invasion of the Israelites would account for many of the destruction levels.

Palestine in the fifteenth and fourteenth centuries B.C. was a land bustling with activity. In addition to the military activity already described, there was increased interest in trade which resulted in the establishment of new contacts with the Western Mediterranean world. New kinds of pottery which were imported from various parts of the Mediterranean began to make an appearance during this period. This was an age of literary activity. In addition to the Amarna letters, we have the significant writings of the people of Ugarit (Ras Shamra) located in the coastal region of Lebanon. These tablets give a rather comprehensive picture of the mythology of these people and significant insight into their religious ideas. It appears that their gods were the same gods as the Canaanites'. The immoral character of their deities led the devotees into the most demoralizing rites found anywhere in the Ancient Near East. Some of these practices included sacred prostitution of both sexes, serpent worship and at times the sacrifice of infants. It is not difficult to see why God issued the command to exterminate the people of the land. The total destruction of the cities of these idolatrous peoples was to prevent the infiltration of these practices into Israel.

B. *The Right of Conquest*

That Israel was to have a land of her own is a clear teaching of Scripture. Over five hundred years before the exodus the Lord promised Abraham that after a period of affliction his seed would be freed and have great possessions (Gen. 15:13-14). In addition to this they would be "given" the land between "the river of Egypt" and the "river Euphrates" (Gen. 15:18). Later, special instructions were given to Moses regarding conquest and settlement of the land (Deut. 7:1-26; 20:1-20). One should always keep in mind that the directive to conquer Canaan was not human but divine.

II. THE BIBLICAL RECORD

A. *Introduction to Joshua*

1. *Position in the Canon*

The Hebrew Old Testament is divided into three sections known as the Law (*torāh*), the prophets (*nebî'îm*) and the writings (*ketubîm*). The Law consists of the five books of Moses. The prophets are divided into two sections, the former and latter prophets (see chart below). The writings contain the poetical books, the five rolls and some historical books.

Law	Prophets		Writings	
Five Books of Moses	Former Josh. — Kings	Latter Isa. — Mal.	Poetical Five Rolls Historical	(3 Books) (5 Books) (3 Books)

2. *The Title of the Book*

The book is named after its principal character, Joshua (Heb. *yehošua'*). The name means "Jehovah saves" or "Jehovah is salvation." The title of the book in the Septuagint[7] is *Iesous Naun*, "Joshua the son of Nun."

3. *The Author*

The liberal-critical view of authorship is that Joshua represents the work of several writers. The two main sources of this book are traced to two supposed documents, J (850 B.C.) and E (750 B.C.). These two documents were assumed to have been re-edited in 650 B.C. and again in 550 B.C. The final form of the book, according to the liberal view, is to be dated to the middle of the sixth century B.C.[8] This view is unnecessary and without real objective proof. Since the book appears as a literary unit, it is better to assume a single author rather than many authors. It is our view that the author of the book was Joshua himself, although some additions were evidently made after his death. The following are the reasons for assuming Joshua as the principal author of the book: (1) The author was an eyewitness to many of the events (Josh. 5:1, 6; 16:4, note the detailed description of the battle for Ai, chaps. 7, 8). The writer speaks of himself as one of those who had crossed over Jordan (5:1) and to whom the land had been promised. (2) Certain parts of the book are said to have been written by

---

7Ancient Greek translation of the Old Testament prepared between 250-150 B.C.

8For a full discussion and evaluation of the Documentary theory of the Pentateuch, see John J. Davis, "The Patriarchs Knowledge of Jehovah," *Grace Journal,* 1963, Vol. 4, No. 1.

Joshua himself (Josh. 24:26, cf. 8:32). (3) Rahab was still living at the time of writing (6:25). (4) Since the Jebusites are described as being in control of Jerusalem (15:63), the book must have been written before the time of David, for David drove the Jebusites out and took full control of that city (II Sam. 5:5-9). (5) The Philistines do not appear as a particular menace in Joshua's time. This would seem to reflect a period prior to the great Philistine invasion of the southwest coasts of Palestine in the twelfth century B.C.

4. Purpose of the Book

The purpose of the Book of Joshua is to provide an official and authoritative account of God's faithfulness in leading his people into the promised land (cf. Josh. 21:43-45). This book continues the history of Israel begun in the five books of Moses and is an important link in the chain of God's plan of salvation for man.

5. Important Themes in the Book

The Book of Joshua contains at least four important theological themes which have practical values for today. First, the book is a lesson on the covenant faithfulness of Jehovah. The power of God was not only declared in covenant agreement, but also demonstrated. Secondly, the book demonstrates the importance of the *written word of God* (Josh. 1:8; 8:32-35; 23:6-16; 24:26-27). There was an authoritative body of written Scripture in the days of Joshua and this consisted of the books of Moses. There is no appeal to contemporary customs or oral tradition. Thirdly, the book points out the utter failure of human effort apart from divine directives. When Joshua and the children of Israel were faithful to God's word and His will, there was victory. When they abandoned His will in favor of their own genius, there was failure and frustration. Finally, the book is a commentary on God's holiness and His judgment of sin. The destruction of the cities of Canaan with their inhabitants was not merely to give Israel military control of the area, but it was, in effect, a judgment of God upon the wickedness of that land (cf. Gen. 15:16; Deut. 7:5-6).

6. *Outline of the Book*

III. THE MAN JOSHUA

A. *The Selection of the Man*

While the Bible does not specifically indicate why God chose Joshua for the great responsibility of leading the conquest of Canaan, we do have important information regarding the background and character of the man Joshua which should help us in understanding God's selection. In all probability Joshua was born in the land of Egypt. We know nothing of his parents, but according to Numbers 1:10 and I Chronicles 7:27 his grandfather, Elishama, was a leader of the tribe of Ephraim in the wilderness journey. The first mention of the man Joshua is found in Exodus 17:9, but nothing is given of his background or piety. It is clear from Exodus 33:11 that Joshua was a young man during the time of the wilderness journey. The fact that Moses chose Joshua to lead the Israelite troops against Amalek at Rephidim (Exod. 17:8-13) indicates that he had already distinguished himself in the area of military service. It is possible that Joshua had received some training in Egypt or perhaps had previous experience in military affairs. His later victories in the land of Canaan seem to support this assumption. According to Scripture, Joshua was the only adult Israelite of the exodus, with the exception of Caleb, who survived the forty years of wandering and actually entered Canaan.

Perhaps the outstanding characteristic of the man Joshua was his unqualified courage. This was demonstrated when he and eleven other spies returned from examining the fortified cities of southern Canaan. Joshua and Caleb stood alone in their evaluation of that situation. The ten spies contended that the children of Israel were in fact "like grasshoppers" when compared with the might of the Canaanites (Num. 13:33). The Scripture terms their report an "evil report" (13:32; 14:37). The original for evil has the idea of slanderous report (cf. 14:36). Joshua and Caleb were convinced that in spite of the size of the enemy the Lord was fully capable of giving them victory (Num. 14:9). This was not an easy position to take, for the whole nation turned against them, and God had to bring a severe judgment upon His people (Num. 14:12, 29 ff.). The account, none the less, indicates that Joshua was fully convinced that the Lord was able to care for any situation that might arise. He was not only a man of faith and courage, but he was also a man of unqualified obedience both to Moses his superior and to the Lord (cf. Exod. 17:8-10; 24:13-18 with Exod. 32:15-18; note also Num. 13 and Heb. 11:30). The real success of Joshua, however, probably lies in the fact that he was a Spirit-filled man (Num. 27:18; cf. Deut. 34:9). Joshua's submission to the leadership of the Holy Spirit caused him to have a high respect for the will of God as revealed in the written Word of God. This obedience and respect, of course, led to victory in all areas of his life.

B. *The Preparation of the Man*

It appears from the early chapters of Joshua and certain references in Numbers and Deuteronomy that Joshua was prepared by God in three ways.

1. *Experience*

You can explain to a man the various techniques of swimming, and that man might develop into a thorough scholar of the theory of buoyancy and stroke techniques. He may have read all of the books available in various types of competitive swimming, but if that man had never been in the water, it is doubtful that he would be much of a swimmer. He must have experience, not merely theory. Such is the case with Joshua. Very early in Joshua's career, he was exposed to circumstances and problems which would help him develop in character and commitment. He was faced with difficult, if not impossible, military situations. This caused him, at the outset, to trust the Lord and seek divine guidance from the "captain of the Lord's host." It has been said many times that experience is a good teacher but needs a willing pupil. From what we can observe in the life of Joshua, he was a willing pupil. The second way in which God prepares a man for His service is by example.

2. *Example*

Joshua had the unique opportunity of serving as "Moses' minister" (Josh. 1:1; Exod. 24:13). This gave Joshua the opportunity to observe the aged statesman of Israel who was over eighty years old during the time of journeying. He was able to observe Moses in times of victory and tribulation (e.g., the exodus from Egypt, Exod. 11, 12; the crossing of the Red Sea, Exod. 14). He was also able to witness the reaction and the response of Moses in times of great frustration and distress (Num. 14:12-23). Moses had learned the important lessons of prayer and intercession. When difficulties arose which he could not handle, he turned to the Lord and sought divine guidance. By being Moses' minister, Joshua quickly learned what the issues really were in national leadership. He was taught that the greatest enemy of Israel was not necessarily the great armies located in the land of Canaan, but could be the subtle deception of Satan *within* the nation of Israel. A case in point would be the tragic description of idolatry recorded in Exodus 32 and 33. On this occasion, Moses had gone up into the mountain and while there, the people, supported by Aaron the priest, decided to make their own gods (Exod. 32:1). They not only made false gods and a molten calf, but they built an altar to these gods and proclaimed special feast days (Exod. 32:5). Joshua was able to witness the broken heart of Moses as he descended from the mountain and saw the people worshiping the very gods which had been proven worthless through the ten plagues in Egypt. According to Exodus 32:17 it was Joshua who heard the noise of the people as they sang and shouted to the false gods. He was also able to witness the anger and holy indignation of Moses as he looked upon the sensuous activity of the Israelites around the golden calf. Joshua certainly must have understood that leadership over this nation would mean standing alone and depending solely on God's power and His word. Joshua not only learned the lesson of obedience from the life of Moses, but he also learned that disobedience would bring the judgment of God. Moses, of course, did not enter the Promised Land because of such disobedience.

The final means by which God prepares a man for His service is through exhortation.

3. *Exhortation*

Joshua was the recipient of considerable special and direct revelation from God. He was not in the dark with regard to what God wanted him to do. He had the exhortations of the Lord as recorded in the five books of Moses. These books were in written form and had full authority. When he was commissioned to take the leadership of the people of Israel, he was reminded that the key to success was meditation in, and complete obedience to, God's revelation (Josh. 1:8).

We should observe at this point that while the program of God is different today, the preparation of the man of God is essentially the same. One learns by experience. The tragedies and the joys of the Christian life cause us to mature in the faith and depend more upon the power of God. The believer learns by the example of others, especially the record of those lives given to us in the Word of God. Observe what the Apostle Paul said about the example of Old Testament saints in I Corinthians 10:11, ". . . all these things happened unto them for examples;

and they are written for our admonition upon whom the ends
of the world are come" (cf. Rom. 15:4). And finally, the believer learns by exhortations found in the Word of God. He is
not without spiritual and practical directives. If he meditates
in the Word of God as commanded, he has every right to anticipate progress and victory.

C. *The Success of the Man*

That Joshua was a successful leader cannot be doubted. He
took a new generation of Israelites and led them to the east
bank of the Jordan. They were confronted with a flooding Jordan River, a well-equipped enemy, rugged and unknown hill
country, and well-fortified cities. In spite of this, Joshua was
able to accomplish spectacular victories and a very successful
conquest of large amounts of territory. This is not just due to
the military or tactical genius of Joshua, but it is due to his unqualified obedience to God who brought victory and success.
Such obedience is not optional for the believer; it is mandatory.
Perhaps one of the reasons believers experience limited success
in spiritual warfare today is because their obedience to our
Lord is halfhearted. The army of the church sometimes marches
slowly and indecisively. In this age of confusion and indecision,
the believer needs more than ever to examine the example
set by the man Joshua. He needs to return to a recognition of
the authority of the Word of God; then he "will prosper and
have good success."

Chapter 2

PREPARING TO CONQUER
(Joshua 1–5)

After forty years of disillusionment, death, and despair the children of Israel finally reached the eastern banks of the Jordan River. For the first time they could see the Promised Land of which their fathers spoke. To see the land is one thing, but to conquer it another. Such conquest would require inspired leadership, divine help, and personal consecration on the part of every Israelite. Such preparation would in effect be the key to victory for both Israel and Joshua.

This chapter will deal with Israel's *entrance* into the land of Canaan. This subject has two phases: (1) preparations for entrance into the land, and (2) the crossing of the Jordan.

I. JOSHUA'S COMMISSION (1:1-9)

The first verse in the Book of Joshua sets the stage for the events that are to follow. Three important facts are given to us in this verse. We are told that Moses was dead. Moses here is described as "the servant of the Lord." This expression is significant because it gives us further insight into the character and ministry of the man Moses. The expression is used two ways in the Old Testament: (1) to describe a pious Israelite who worshipped the true God (Lev. 25:42, 55; Isa. 41:8; 43:10) and (2) to describe one with a special call or commission (II Chron. 32:16; Gen. 26:24; II Sam. 3:18). This verse informs us that Joshua was the "minister" of Moses. This position included two basic responsibilities: (1) military and (2) religious (cf. Exod. 24:13; Num. 27:18-23; Deut. 1:38; 31:23). Finally, this verse indicates the source of Joshua's commission; namely, Jehovah, the God of Israel (cf. Num. 27:18; Deut. 31:3-7, 23; 34:9).

A. *The Promise of the Land* (1:2-7)

In the remaining verses dealing with the Lord's promise of the land, three things stand out as significant: (1) *the promise of divine support* (v. 2). Jehovah clearly indicated that He was already in the process or was "about to give" them the land before them (Heb. *'ānokî notēn*). This expression should be compared to a similar one found in verse three where the Hebrew is different. It is translated in the Authorized Version ". . . that have I given you" (Heb. *lākem netatîw*). The expression in verse two points to the immediate help of the Lord, whereas in verse three the emphasis is upon divine finality. As far as God was concerned, the land was already theirs and needed only to be possessed. (2) *The indication of geographic scope* (vv. 3-5). These verses are important because they give to us the general boundaries of Israel's possession. Every part of the land on which they would march the Lord would give to them (cf. Exod. 23:30-31). According to the third verse, this would include the area from the wilderness "unto this Lebanon even to the great River Euphrates" (cf. Deut. 11:24). These expressions give us an indication of the northernmost territories of Israel's possession, which possession included "the land of the Hittites." This expression is usually regarded as referring to the land of Syria which, of course, was under Hittite control at certain times.[9] The western boundary of the Promised Land includes all the territory unto "the great sea toward the going down of the sun," a reference to the Mediterranean coast. (3) *Some personal admonitions* (vv. 5-7). The Lord promised Joshua that as He supported and strengthened Moses, so He would strengthen him (Deut. 11:25, also Deut. 7:24; Heb. 13:5-6; I Sam. 14:6; Rom. 8:31). The last expression in verse five is interesting. He says there, "I will not fail thee." The Hebrew (*rāpāh*) literally means to be weak. The expression might well be translated, "I will not drop" or "abandon thee." In the light of this promise Joshua was encouraged to be "strong and of good courage" (vv. 6, 7; cf. v. 9). Personal courage and consistent obedience to the will of God will secure for Joshua and the children of Israel prosperity, but full prosperity is only realized when there is complete obedience to the Word of God. This leads us to the next point of emphasis in Joshua's commission.

---

[9]This expression is omitted in the LXX and in Deuteronomy 11:24.

B. *The Power of the Word* (1:8)

Many critics today argue that the Scriptures never really appeared in authoritative, written form until after the ninth century B.C. This view, however, is purely speculative and in contradiction to clear statements of Scripture. Verse 8 in this chapter clearly indicates that in the fourteenth century B.C. there was a "book of the law" which was not only recognized as revelatory in nature, but authoritative (cf. Exod. 17:14; 24: 4, 7; Deut. 31:9, 11, 24, 26). Joshua is commanded to meditate day and night in this book and to observe the truths that are taught therein. One should notice also the emphasis upon the word "written" found in this verse. We are talking about a written body of literature which carries with it full divine approval and authority. This verse regards the Word of God as the key to prosperity and success (cf. Ps. 1:1-3; I Kings 2:3). The critical proposition that Scripture is the product of oral tradition surviving many hundreds of years of transmission is not only questionable on historical grounds, but highly improbable from a practical point of view. In addition to this, it should be noted that the Book of Joshua puts specific emphasis on the *written law of Moses* and its importance within the economy of Israel (cf. Josh. 8:32-35; 24:25-27). Our text does not merely require knowledge of the law, but daily meditation in it. Meditation involves mature reflection upon the Word of God and its place in one's life. This practice is the basis of spiritual growth and true progress in practical godliness (cf. Ps. 1:1-3; 119:15, 97).

C. *The Presence of the Lord* (1:9)

When the Lord Jesus sent out His disciples to proclaim the gospel to the ends of the world, one of the things He emphasized was the promise of His personal presence wherever they would go (Matt. 28:19-20). Joshua was also commanded to move out and to conquer in the name of Yahweh. It is therefore significant that He too was promised the special presence of the Lord (cf. Josh. 3:7; Deut. 31:6-8).

II. PREPARATIONS FOR THE JORDAN CROSSING (1:10—2:24)

The actual chronology of events recorded in the first three

chapters of Joshua is somewhat difficult to organize. For example, 1:11 speaks of the possibility of crossing over the Jordan within three days. Then in 2:22 we are told that the spies spent at least three days in the mountains having made a covenant with Rahab. Finally, in 3:2 we are informed that after three days "the officers went through the host." The question is, "How much time actually transpired between the initial phases of preparation for the Jordan crossing and the actual crossing of the river described in Chapter 3?" Some commentators suggest the following order of events for Chapters 1-3: (1) The spies are sent out (chap. 2); (2) tribal preparation follows (1:10-18), and (3) preparations for the march (3:2 ff.). Other scholars feel that 1:10 and 3:2 actually are describing synonymous events, and Chapter 2 is really parenthetical. The spy mission is regarded as having begun before the events of 1:10. Either of these views is chronologically possible.

A. *Tribal Responsibilities* (1:10-18)

The immediate problem facing Joshua was the organization of the tribes and preparation of food for the journey to Canaan. Joshua gathered his officers together to give them specific instructions as to how the people should prepare for this journey (vv. 10, 11). The expression "officers of the people" (Heb. *šoṭerê hā'ām*) literally refers to scribes. In all probability these were scribes of the military role (muster). Perhaps these are parallel to today's staff officers who issue the administrative orders of a command.[10] Reuben, Gad, and the half tribes of Manasseh were clearly reminded of their military responsibility to the rest of the nation (1:12-18). Moses had earlier given them permission to settle on the east bank of the Jordan River as long as they fulfilled their military responsibility with regard to conquest of the land of Canaan (Num. 32). This obligation was upon them until their brothers had "rest" in the land (v. 13). To this they agreed without qualification (vv. 16-18).

B. *Rahab and the Spies* (2:1-24)

The preparations for, and organization of, a spy mission were

---

[10]On this term, see Exodus 5:6-19; Deuteronomy 1:15; I Chronicles 27:1.

not new to the man Joshua. He had participated in a rather
crucial spy mission from Kadesh-barnea (Num. 13-14). Because
of that tragic experience in which the spies were permitted to
give their report publicly, Joshua decided that this mission should
be conducted "secretly" (2:1). He had learned by experience
that spy reports should be brought to the leaders only, for the
people did not have sufficient orientation or experience to
properly evaluate such a report. Because of the proximity of
the tribes of Israel to Jericho, it was necessary that this spy mission be carried out with as little commotion as possible. Surely
the inhabitants of Jericho were anticipating such a mission. The
job given to the spies was not an easy one. Jericho was located in an open valley. It was a walled city, and the people
in the city were keenly aware of the danger from without.
In addition to these problems we are informed that the Jordan
was in the flood stage, overflowing its banks (3:15; 4:18; I
Chron. 12:15). This meant that the spies probably had to travel
some distance north, cross the Jordan, and then come southward
probably entering Jericho from the west side. This would be not
only advantageous for them in that they would have the cover
of the caves in the mountains to the west of Jericho, but the
king of Jericho would least suspect a spy mission from that direction. Upon entering Jericho, they came to the house of Rahab
who was described as a harlot (v. 1). Josephus, however, pre-
fers to regard her as an innkeeper.[11] This view, however, even
though shared by some modern commentators, does not seem
to be the best in the light of the original text and New Testament references.[12]

From the verses and chapters that follow quite a bit can
be ascertained about the city of Jericho. For example, we learn,
at least by implication, that it was a sinful city (2:1). Secondly,
the city had sophisticated political organization, for it had a
king (2:2). According to 2:5, 15 it was a walled city with a
gate and therefore well fortified. In the fourth place the record
indicates that houses were built on and along the wall (2:15).

---

[11]*Ant.* V: 8:2, 7.

[12]The Hebrew word is *zonāh*, compare the Greek *pornē* (Heb. 11:31;
James 2:25). .

This, of course, was customary for houses not only in this period but in the Middle Bronze Age as well. In the fifth place, there is the implication that Jericho had contact with other nations. One of the items discovered at Jericho was a "goodly Babylonish garment" (7:21). This phrase might better be translated "one beautiful mantle from Shinar." This would seem to imply that Jericho had some trade contact with the Tigris-Euphrates cultural milieu. Finally, the text informs us that Jericho had an army (6:2). The size and strength of this army is not indicated in the text, but because of the detailed preparations undertaken by Joshua for this mission, we might assume that the city presented a formidable fighting force.

As the two Israelite spies began questioning Rahab, they immediately became aware of the fact that they had come in contact with one who was knowledgeable of both the history of Israel and the attitude of the Canaanites. For example, she had heard about the crossing of the Red Sea and the great victories accomplished on the east side of the Jordan (v. 10). The Canaanites at this time were very much afraid of the power of Israel and her God. In the light of this fear she requested a personal covenant with them that she and her family might be saved when Israel invaded the land (vv. 12 ff.). The spies agreed that if she gave them accurate information and maintained secrecy regarding their mission, she and her family would indeed be rescued, providing they remained in her house at the time of conquest (vv. 18-19). While the spies were speaking with Rahab, the king of Jericho received word of their presence in the city. A contingent of soldiers was sent immediately to the house of Rahab, and they demanded that the spies be turned over to them. In the meantime, Rahab had hidden the spies on the roof of her house (v. 6). To the soldiers she replied that, yes, the spies had come to her, but she did not know where they were (v. 4). This, of course, was a lie which brings to light a rather interesting problem. Was the lie of Rahab justified? After all, she uttered the lie in defense of two innocent Israelites. If she would have given the truth, would not both of these men have been killed by the king of Jericho? This problem has plagued modern commentators. Modern theologians tend to justify the lie of Rahab by what is commonly called "situational ethics"; that is, in this particular situation the lie was justified. This leads us to another important question, "Does the end really justify the means?" This is not the first time that a lie was uttered in the protection of another. Remember Abraham's lie (Gen. 12, 20). There are other parallel situations in Scripture which indicate that this was a problem to the people of this time.[13] Rahab probably did not see evil in her act. She saw the situation as a choice between two evils — being responsible for these two men who came from Israel, or to lie and save them. However, it is clear from Scripture that God regards all lies as evil and sinful. For one to lie in this manner is for one to assume that he knows the outcome of a situation which, in fact, he does not. God has control of every situation and therefore it might well be the will of God that the spies should die. It is the job of the believer to represent the truth and allow the Lord to care for that situation.

When the spies returned to Joshua, they brought a rather optimistic report to him. It is clear that they accepted the evaluation of Rahab without question. They were convinced not only of the fear of the Canaanites, but they were also convinced of the Lord's provision for them (vv. 23-24).

III. CROSSING THE JORDAN RIVER (3:1–5:15)

A. *Organization for the Crossing* (3:1-4)

Immediately after the return of the spies, Joshua began preparations for the crossing of the Jordan. The immediacy of Joshua's action is interesting. It indicates that he fully believed in the provision of the Lord. When the time came to actually move toward Jordan, Joshua did not request an extension of time in order to let the Jordan subside. He did not plead for a different route so as to avoid confrontation with the enemy. He did not call for a caucus, a commission, or a committee report in five copies, with this committee to be duly organized and named "The Committee on Crisis in the Contemporary Situation." Without argument and without delay, he prepared to march. The officers went through the tribes, and as they did,

---

[13]Genesis 26; I Samuel 19:14; Exodus 1:15-22; Genesis 31:33-35.

they commanded that the ark should be kept in view. There was to be a space between the ark and the people of about 2,000 cubits (v. 4). This would mean that there was a space around the ark of about 3,000 feet. There are probably two reasons why this was done: (1) in order that all the people might be able to see the ark, and to understand that it was God who was leading them into the land, and not a great military force, and (2) because of the sacredness of the ark.

B. *Consecration for the Crossing* (3:5-13)

Another indication that the march of Israel was not merely a military exploit, but a spiritual fulfillment, is given in verse 5 of this chapter. The people were not commanded at this point to prepare their swords and shields but to prepare themselves. They were commanded to "sanctify themselves" (3:5, cf. 7:13). This sanctification was not ceremonial but spiritual. They were commanded to set themselves apart for God's program and will. They were ordered to keep their eyes on the Ark of the Covenant for leadership in the march, not the soldiers, the generals, or even Joshua. After Joshua gave the command to march, the Lord again spoke to him and reaffirmed His promise to be with Joshua and give him victory.

C. *The Completion of the Crossing* (3:14-17)

This particular event has given rise to considerable speculation among various Bible commentators. The Scriptures tell us that the priests went down to the waters of the Jordan, which at this time were rushing southward toward the Dead Sea in flood stage. They dipped their feet in the brim of the water (v. 15), and when that happened, the waters were stopped; that is, according to verse 16, they were heaped up in one heap at the city of Adam which is near Zaretan. The Authorized Version at this point is weak. Rather than the translation "very far from the city of Adam" it should read "at the city of Adam." This would mean that the waters were stopped at approximately thirteen to fifteen miles north of the Dead Sea. This would, of course, permit a wide expanse for the children of Israel to cross. Adam has generally been identified with Tell el-Damiyeh, about fifteen miles north of the Jericho area. Zaretan has been

The Jordan River.
Matson Photo Service

identified as the site of Tell es-Sa'idiyeh, which is located approximately twelve miles north of Adam.

The nature of this event has been brought in question in recent years. There are at least three views regarding the character of the event as described in Scripture. There are those who deny the whole event as being purely fictitious. Others assert that God used a natural phenomenon; that is, an earthquake actually caused the crumbling of some of the cliffs in the northern part of the Jordan thereby blocking the waters and permitting Israel to cross. There is some precedence for such a view. On December 8, A.D. 1267, a large section of the west bank of the river fell into the river, stopping its flow for approximately sixteen hours. Again on July 11, 1927, a landslide near the ford at Damiyeh was caused by an earthquake, and the flow was blocked for twenty-one hours. While such an event is possible, one must agree that the timing would have to be a miracle. Furthermore, these did not occur at the flood season, whereas the Biblical event did (cf. 3:15; 4:18).

The third view is that the event should be regarded as basically supernatural in nature, that is; the Lord, by causes unknown to us, stopped the flow of the Jordan for a sufficient amount of time to enable the Israelites to cross safely. It is unlikely that the Lord would employ something as destructive as an earthquake merely to stop the flow of a river. Furthermore, an earthquake in the Jordan valley would have endangered Israelite settlements on the east bank (cf. 3:1). It might also be noted that the Jordan was stopped on two later occasions in order to permit passage (cf. II Kings 2:8, 14). Are we to assume that two successive earthquakes occurred merely to permit the prophets to cross? With the facts we have at present, it is the better part of wisdom not to attempt to provide natural causes for what appears to be a special act of God in behalf of His people.

D. *The Commemoration of the Crossing* (4:1-24)

The Lord commanded that two memorials be established to commemorate the miracle of the Jordan crossing. One man from each of the tribes was to carry a stone out of the Jordan, and this would be used for a special memorial on the west bank of this river. In actuality, two memorials were established to commemorate this event. The one which is described in verses 9-18, was actually placed in the Jordan River. The other was situated near or in the camp of Gilgal. This is described in verses 20-24. The memorials were designed to perpetuate the memory of this miraculous crossing. The Lord was concerned that future generations would have an appreciation of God's provision for His people (cf. vv. 21-23). The memorial served not only as a commemoration of God's provision for His own people, but they were evidently designed to be a sign of God's power to the nations around about (v. 24). According to this chapter, all the tribes participated in the crossing. The two and a half tribes sent representative armies with the rest of the nation (vv. 12-13). Verse 13 indicates that 40,000 men of the two and a half tribes actually crossed over the Jordan. It is clear from Numbers 26:7, 18, and 34 that the total potential fighting force of these tribes numbered about 110,580 men. Why, then, did only 40,-000 cross over? The answer is probably found in the situation on the east bank. The conquest might take some time, and the eastern tribes could not afford to leave their cities undefended. We might presume therefore that the remaining parts of their armies stayed on the east side for purposes of local protection.

E. *Circumcision after the Crossing* (5:1-15)

The words found in verse 1 of this chapter are in effect a clear fulfillment of the promises given in Exodus 23:27. They also confirm the evaluation of Rahab recorded in the second chapter of this book. It is appropriate that as they stand in the new land that there should be a renewal of a very important covenant practice. Evidently the practice of circumcision was abandoned during the wilderness journey. Verse 2 describes this as the second circumcision with respect to the exodus. There are two views as to why this important rite was neglected. Some argue that God did not permit them to perform this rite because of their sin (cf. v. 6).[14] According to Numbers 14:29, all Is-

---

[14]Compare John Rea, "Joshua," *The Wycliffe Bible Commentary*. Charles F. Pfeiffer and Everett F. Harrison, eds. (Chicago: Moody Press, 1962), p. 211.

raelites twenty years and older were condemned to die in the wilderness. This was thirty-eight years before they reached the Jordan River. This means, therefore, that all males under the age of thirty-eight were uncircumcised, and those between the ages of thirty-eight and fifty-seven were circumcised before they left Egypt (cf. v. 5).

Joshua was commanded to make "knives of flint."[15] All Is-raelites who had not been circumcised were therefore to par-ticipate in this important covenant sign, and with participation should come a renewed commitment to the covenant given to Abraham (Gen. 15-17). On the fourteenth day of this month, the children of Israel kept the Passover (v. 10). One day later they ate of the food of the land, and finally, on the sixteenth day of that month, the manna which had sustained them the forty years in the wilderness ceased to be provided (v. 12).

As the Lord appeared to Moses in a special way to prepare him for leadership (Exod. 3:2), so the Lord appeared to Joshua in a similar manner (5:13-15). Joshua did not immediately rec-ognize his visitor as a divine being (v. 13); but as the Lord spoke to him, His identity became clear, and Joshua fell down and worshiped Him, and that without rebuke (v. 14). This special appearance of the Lord was not merely to encourage Joshua, but was to convey important information which he would need in the conquest of Jericho. It is especially significant that Joshua was commanded to remove the sandals from off his feet as Moses had to do in a similar situation (v. 15, cf. Exod. 3:5). This encounter was designed to give specific instruction for the conquest of the city of Jericho. It is the view of this author that the conversation begun in the latter verses of Chapter 5 is con-tinued in 6:2, with verse 1 being a brief parenthetical statement.

One can only imagine the tremendous excitement that must have characterized the camp of Israel on this occasion. There was probably activity in every area as the tribes organized, set up the camps, and as the leaders attempted to plan for the fu-ture. Finally, they had reached the shores of the land that had been promised to their fathers. While there must have been an air of rejoicing and thanksgiving, there probably was also

---

[15]Hebrew *ḥarḇoṯ ṣurîm* cf. Exod. 4:25).

considerable concern about the future of this expedition. They had not really encountered the enemy up to this point. Before them lay the walled city of Jericho with its imposing defensive systems. The real tests still lay ahead.

Chapter 3

THE FIRST ENCOUNTER
(Joshua 6)

Scarcely had the dust from the massive Israelite encampment settled in the Gilgal area when the Israelites realized that the Jordan crossing and the reinstitution of certain covenant practices were merely first steps in the fulfillment of God's promise. To the south of them lay the city of Jericho with its impressive defensive systems. Further to the west lay the great mountains of central Palestine. Before the tribes could even think of settlement in this vast expanse of land, Jericho had to be taken. The following discussion will deal with that problem and the solution that Joshua employed.

I. THE PROMISE OF VICTORY (6:1-2)

A. *Literary Structure*

As indicated in the last chapter, it appears that verse 1 of this chapter is parenthetical and verse 2, in effect, carries on the conversation between Joshua and the "captain of the Lord's host" (5:13-15). The purpose of this parenthetical statement is to explain the immediate situation (6:2-5). So great was the fear of the invading Israelites that the defenders of Jericho shut the gate to the city not permitting any traffic in or out of the city (v. 1). After the successful visit of the spies, it is easy to understand why such action was taken.

B. *The Certainty of Victory* (v. 2)

Jehovah again reminded Joshua that victory was assured because of divine intervention. The expression "I have given" is an exclamation of prophetic certainty (cf. Heb. *nātatî*). The scope of victory is also indicated in this verse. The city, the king, and the army would all fall into the hands of Israel according to God's promise.

II. THE BATTLE PLAN (6:3-7)

A. *The Nature of the Plan*

To say the least, the battle plan revealed to Joshua was most unusual. It was indeed an act of faith on the part of Joshua to propose such a plan to the seasoned generals representing the various tribes. There is no evidence of rebellion to the plan as presented by Joshua, however, which probably indicates the commitment of the military leaders under Joshua to the Lord. The march around the walls was to be characterized by silence (6:10) except for the blowing of the rams' horns (6:8). They were to march around the walls of the city once each day and seven times on the last day at which time the walls would collapse, giving them access to the city of Jericho (6:3-5).

B. *The Purpose of the Plan*

The purpose of such a battle plan was probably twofold. (1) It was designed to test Israel's obedience to the will of God. A march like this would only bring ridicule from the enemy — at least in the early phases. Israel would have to humble herself and remain in complete submission to God's proposals — a very important lesson in this stage of the conquest of Canaan. (2) The plan was obviously designed to strike fear into the heart of the enemy. The defenders of Jericho were already in a state of frustration because of the previous victories of Israel (cf. 2:9-11). The march around the city in military formation, yet without any attempt to attack must have sent "the Jericho commission on defense" into a number of special late evening sessions! The culmination of this march would be the collapse of Jericho's walls and subsequent destruction of the city (v. 5).

III. THE FALL OF JERICHO (6:8-27)

A. *The March around the Walls* (6:8-19)

This section of Chapter 6 deals with the organization of the march and the manner in which it was carried out over the seven-day period. It is quite clear that the march was not

Air View of the Plain of Jericho. The ancient mound of Jericho (Tell es-Sultan) in the foreground. Modern Jericho lies further distant. The Dead Sea and Mountains of Moab in the background (Joshua 3-6). Matson Photo Service

merely military in nature but religious. The prominent place given to the priests and the ark indicate that it was God who was leading them into battle and victory, and not Joshua or the soldiers of the nation of Israel. A single march around the nine acre mound area probably took twenty-five to thirty-five minutes. It should not be concluded that every Israelite took part in this march. Such a feat would not only be impractical, but would be impossible. It is more probable to assume that the march was carried out by tribal representation. Such seems to be the battle procedure even in the conquest to follow. The order of march is given in verses 7-9, 13. The chart below illustrates the general order of march as indicated in these verses.

ORGANIZATION OF THE MARCH

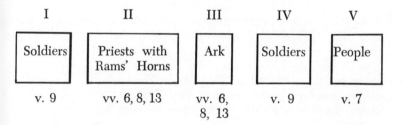

I	II	III	IV	V
Soldiers	Priests with Rams' Horns	Ark	Soldiers	People
v. 9	vv. 6, 8, 13	vv. 6, 8, 13	v. 9	v. 7

We are not given the details of each day's activities, but can assume that the early part of the week brought considerable ridicule from the inhabitants of Jericho. However, as the days passed, and the army continued to march in confidence, a gross silence probably came over the defenders of that city. When would Israel attack? What type of strategy were they using? It was probably not easy for the leaders of Israel to remain silent early in the week when the enemy ridiculed their faith and their intentions, but as is the case in every generation, when men act upon the promises of God with complete faith, victory is theirs.

Joshua instructed the people that the city of Jericho was accursed (vv. 17, 18). The Hebrew term translated "accurse" (Heb.

ḥērem) means to "ban, devote, or exterminate." It may also mean to "seclude from society." This term was applied to capital punishment (Lev. 27:29), to offerings given to God (Ezek. 44:29; Num. 18:14), and with reference to "the utter destruction" of the enemies of God (Isa. 34:5; Deut. 7:26; 20:17). It is also used spiritually of God's judgment against impenitent sinners (Mal. 4:6). This expression means, therefore, that Jericho and all of its contents were completely devoted to Jehovah as the firstfruits of the land, for a sign that they would receive all Canaan from Him. Joshua made it clear that no objects were to be kept by any of the invading Israelites (v. 18). The exception to this prohibition is found in the nineteenth verse. Silver, gold, and the vessels of bronze and iron were to be kept and consecrated unto the Lord as part of His treasury (v. 19).

B. *The Collapse of the Walls* (6:20-21)

As the people completed their march on that important seventh day, they shouted when the priests gave the signal with the rams' horns (v. 20). It was at this time that the walls of Jericho collapsed in place . The literal rendering of the Hebrew is "the wall fell in its place." The question frequently raised concerning this event "Why did the walls of Jericho fall?" To this question, many answers have been given. For example, there is the popular view that an earthquake occurred at just the right moment. While this is entirely possible, it would still require a miracle of timing. Indeed, an earthquake of such magnitude to destroy the walls of an established city might be one which would bring some destruction to the encampment of Gilgal located rather near to the city of Jericho. More bizarre is the viewpoint that sound waves caused the walls to crumble. One writer suggests that the pitch of the trumpets and the shout of the individuals caused tremendous vibrations, thereby bringing about the collapse of the walls. Others have suggested that the children of Israel marched in step causing great shock waves beneath the walls and thus caused the walls to crumble. Some have suggested that the walls were built on sandy soil and were already in cracked condition. The vibrations from the shouting, the rams' horns, and the stomping of feet were the things that caused the walls finally to collapse. Such views, while attractive to the general public, do not really solve any problems. The wall construction at Jericho was not haphazard, as excavations have shown. It is extremely doubtful, in any event, that the pitch of rams' horns or the united voices of the people would really have any effect upon the massive mud brick walls of that ancient city. It is better to assume that God himself brought about, by supernatural means, the collapse of these walls. Otherwise, we have no way of accounting for the fact that most sections of the wall collapsed except those that surrounded the house of Rahab, for as long as Rahab and her family remained in her house, according to the agreement with the spies (2:17-20), she would be safe from the destruction that was to come to Jericho. This promise was fulfilled as recorded in verse 22 of this chapter. While the walls of the city collapsed destroying the houses adjacent to it, the house of Rahab remained intact, thereby preserving her and her family.

C. *Archaeology and the Fall of Jericho*

The archaeological evidence from Jericho (Tell es-Sultan) is not clear regarding the destruction of this city by Joshua. The excavations conducted at the site, between 1930 and 1936, by John Garstang indicated that the city was extensively occupied down to the year 1550 B.C. This occupation was recorded by Garstang as being that of the Hyksos peoples. Garstang also discovered another city level which he called City IV, and related this to the Late Bronze Age period, or the period of the conquest. He felt that he had discovered the walls of Jericho dating to Joshua's period. The walls were actually two parallel walls. The inner wall measured about twelve feet thick; the outer wall six feet thick with approximately twelve feet between. It appeared to him that these mud brick walls had been destroyed by an earthquake in connection with an intense fire. Between the years 1952 and 1958, the site was again excavated under the leadership of Miss Kathleen Kenyon. Her work at the site indicated that the walls had been misidentified by Garstang. Rather than the walls belonging to the Late Bronze

Age, they represented a much earlier period (Early Bronze) and were not contemporary walls but, in effect, revealed two separate building phases. This does not mean that all of Garstang's evidence has been negated by the later excavations. Dr. Garstang found some 320 Late Bronze Age objects, including two scarabs of Amenhotep III (1410-1372 B.C.) as well as Late Bronze sherds on the mound. After the destruction of the city, about 1550 B.C., the mound lay vacant for about 150 years. Since most of the typically fifteenth century pottery forms are lacking, it is concluded that reoccupation must have taken place about 1410 B.C. or a little earlier. It is entirely possible that the Canaanites occupying the site in Joshua's day reused parts of the Hyksos' fortifications in building their own mud brick walls. The reason that very little Late Bronze Age material is found at the site is that after its destruction by Joshua, the site remained unoccupied for a long period of time. In the light of the completeness of the destruction brought by Joshua (6:21-24) and the fact that the mound was exposed allowing the process of erosion to destroy much of the evidence, we therefore should not expect a great abundance of material from Joshua's period. It is also possible that local inhabitants removed much of the material after the abandonment of the site. It is significant that Jericho is not mentioned in any of the Amarna tablets. This seems to confirm the Biblical record of its total destruction and subsequent abandonment.

D. *The Death of All Living Things*

Upon entering the city, and after a brief battle (cf. Josh. 24:11), the armies of Israel destroyed "all that was in the city, both man and woman, young and old, and ox, and sheep, and ass, with the edge of the sword" (v. 21). This action has been subjected to considerable criticism on the part of many Biblical scholars. For example, James Muilenburg considers this type of treatment to be somewhat below high ethical norms.[16] He regards it as a transitional stage in Israel's evolutionary develop-

---

[16]James Muilenburg, "The History of the Religion of Israel," *The Interpreter's Bible*. George A. Buttrick, ed. (New York: Abingdon Press, 1952), p. 310.

ment. Paul Heinisch, on the other hand, regards this event as "one of the imperfections of the Old Testament."[17] Rowley asserts that these practices were in direct conflict with the spirit of New Testament truth.[18] According to his view, we have a contradiction in ethical and moral actions between the Old Testament and the New. W. F. Albright in *From Stone Age to Christianity* argues that this event is no more a moral problem than the massacre of the Armenians by the Turks.[19] He assumes that this was just another national struggle.

Still, the morality of the actions described in this chapter have come under severe scrutiny on the part of modern scholars. Is it true that the Israelites unjustly slaughtered "innocent" Canaanites? There are several facts which should be kept in mind when dealing with this problem. First of all, it should be noted that the destruction of Canaanite cities was based on religious, not political or military considerations (Deut. 7:2-6; 12:2-3; 20:10-18). Secondly, the action taken at Jericho (and also at Ai) was done on the basis of *divine command* (Deut. 7:2; Josh. 8:2; Exod. 17:14; Deut. 20:16) and thus involves the moral character of God. If we believe that God is holy and without imperfection, it follows that whatever He commands will be just and right. And, thirdly, it was really *Jehovah* who was destroying these cities and their peoples (Josh. 6:2; 24:8). Israel should merely be regarded as God's instruments of destruction. Fourthly, the *reason* for this command is clearly stated in Scripture and seems to justify the action taken. For example, Deuteronomy 20:18 makes it clear that this demand was designed to preserve the religious purity of the nation of Israel. The destruction of various Canaanite cities should be regarded as a direct judgment from God because of their iniquity (Gen. 15:16-21, cf. Gen. 19). If the Lord thought it necessary to destroy the cities of Sodom and Gomor-

[17]Paul Heinisch, *Theology of the Old Testament* (The Liturgical Press, 1955), p. 214.

[18]H. H. Rowley, *The Rediscovery of the Old Testament* (Philadelphia: The Westminster Press, 1946), p. 32 ff.

[19]W. F. Albright, *From the Stone Age to Christianity* (Baltimore: The Johns Hopkins Press, 1957), p. 280.

rah because of their sin, it is also appropriate that Jericho
should be destroyed because of its iniquity. The means that God
might use is insignificant in such a case. It might also be observed that the destruction of such cities would serve as a visible illustration of God's view of polytheism. Israel, on several
occasions, was warned that if she became like the Canaanites, she
too would be punished (Deut. 28:15 ff.; Josh. 6:18; 24:20).
Therefore, rather than this command and its fulfillment being in
conflict with the New Testament, it is, after all, a complement
to the theological and moral principles of Scripture as a whole.
God is a holy God. He demands that sin be punished. The
Lord reserves the right to punish sin wherever it is found,
whether it be in the immediate destruction of a city or the
condemnation of the sinner at final judgment. It is only by the
mercy and the grace of God that any sinner is permitted to
live his life completely. In fact, He could punish sin upon the
committing of the first act, take the life of that individual, and
still remain a perfectly righteous and holy God.

E. *The Rescue of Rahab* (6:22-25)

The history of Rahab is a remarkable example of the grace
of God operative in the Old Testament period. In spite of her
past life and the lie that she told, she gave true evidence of
her saving faith in God by "having received the spies with
peace" (Heb. 11:31, cf. Josh. 6:17, 25). A further evidence of
this marvelous grace is the fact that her name appears in the
messianic line (Matt. 1:5). The faith of Rahab brought deliverance to her own immediate family as was the case of Noah
and Lot.

F. *The Curse on the City* (6:26-27)

The curse pronounced by Joshua involved the *refortification*
of Jericho, not merely future habitation. The words "foundation"
and "gates" (v. 26) refer to the establishment of a wall around
the city. It is evident from Judges 1:16; 3:13 (cf. Deut. 34:3)
that the city was to some degree reinhabited a short time after
the destruction. This occupation of the site seems to be very
brief and from an archaeological point of view inconsequential.

The first attempt to refortify the city is recorded in I Kings 16:
34. In the days of King Ahab, a man by the name of Hiel
attempted to rebuild the walls of Jericho, and in so doing he
lost two of his sons in fulfillment of the curse pronounced on the
site by Joshua. This curse, therefore, was fulfilled some 500
years after its pronouncement by Joshua. Some have suggested
that this curse may have been removed by the intercession of
Elisha after the time of Hiel (cf. II Kings 2:18-22).

The quick, spectacular, and decisive victory of the children of
Israel at this site caused inhabitants of Canaan to take special
notice of their potential. As was the case with victories on the
eastern side of the Jordan River, word spread rapidly throughout the land of Canaan regarding the miraculous power of the
God of Israel. The secret to success at Jericho was not mere military genius or battle capability. The success of Israel is due to
her unconditioned faith in, and obedience to, the revealed will
of God.

The Ruins of Ancient Jericho from the East (Joshua 6). Matson Photo
Service

Chapter 4

DEFEAT AND VICTORY
(Joshua 7–9)

The history recorded in the seventh chapter of the Book of Joshua represents one of Israel's darkest hours. Up to now, everything has gone smoothly, and the armies of Israel have tasted only victory. But now the scene drastically changes. Their progress is suddenly halted. Defeat, sorrow, and loss characterize the camp of Israel. Let us examine the events which brought about this tragic scene.

I. THE TRAGEDY OF DEFEAT (Josh. 7)

A. *The Source of Defeat* (7:1-5, 10-12)

The events recorded in this chapter can be described as both unexpected and unprecedented. This chapter reveals how victory on the part of God's people can be quickly undermined by disobedience and sin on the part of a single individual. The reason for Israel's defeat at the city of Ai is given to us in the first verse of this chapter which asserts that Israel "committed a trespass." The word for trespass in the original is of special importance. It is a technical term referring to the misappropriation of property which was considered in a sacred category (cf. Lev. 5:15). The trespass, according to this text, had reference to the "accursed thing." The Hebrew term used here for accursed thing is the same as that which is used in Joshua 6:18; therefore, we are dealing with open rebellion to a clearly revealed prohibition given by God. The effects of the sin of Achan and those who followed him are described in verses 2-5.

In preparation for the next phase of Israel's conquest of Canaan, Joshua sent men from Jericho to the city of Ai which is beside Beth-aven. The city of Ai is generally associated with the ancient site of et-Tell. This site is located in the central hill country of Palestine (see map, page 2). It appears that Joshua wasted little time in organizing the spy mission. Notice that the men were sent from Jericho, not Gilgal. Jericho, of course, was the recent place of battle. The men obeyed and went up to the hill country and searched the area surrounding Ai, as well as the city itself, and brought back to Joshua a rather optimistic report regarding their ability to conquer the city. They suggested that only two or three thousand men would be needed to conquer that site (v. 3) since the people of the city were "but a few." Joshua accepted their report as he had done on previous occasions and organized about 3,000 men to take the city. It would appear from the information given in Joshua 8:25 that the spy report was rather accurate. When the city was destroyed, the total slain, including men and women, was 12,000 (8:25). This would seem to indicate an approximate army size of two to four thousand men. The request for 3,000 soldiers, therefore, was not at all unreasonable. However, when the conflict began, the men of Ai had the upper hand from the beginning and were, without a doubt, superior. The Israelite

The Valley of Achor Near Jericho (Joshua 7:26). Matson Photo Service

troops panicked and fled toward the rocky cliffs leading down to the Jordan valley (7:5). Thirty-six men were slain, and the remaining part of the army reached Gilgal in a state of complete humiliation. The hearts of the people "melted and became as water" (v. 5). It is strange indeed that the description which was originally used for the Canaanites about to be defeated now describes the heart attitude of the Israelites (cf. 2:11 with 5:1).

B. *The Sorrow of Defeat* (7:6-9)

Joshua, upon hearing this news, "rent his clothes and fell upon the earth" in disappointment and sorrow before the Lord. He and the elders of Israel put dust upon their heads, a common procedure when demonstrating a feeling of deep sorrow and humilitation (cf. Gen. 37:34; I Sam. 4:12; II Sam. 1:2; 13:31). The cry of Joshua recorded in verse 7 is strangely familiar. It raises a question which, in essence, was raised by unbelieving and murmuring Israel during the wilderness journey (cf. Exod. 16:2-3; Num. 14:2-4). Joshua was concerned not only about the destiny of the people but also about the name of his God (v. 9). The Lord responded to Joshua's questions quickly and decisively, and pointed out to him that the reason for Israel's defeat and humiliation was sin (v. 11). He was commanded to get up from his face and immediately care for this problem. Someone had violated the Lord's regulations concerning the "accursed thing," and because of this, Israel had become accursed (v. 12).

C. *The Solution to Defeat* (7:13-26)

1. *Confession of Sin* (7:13-21)

The first step in restoring fellowship with God was for the people to "sanctify themselves" (v. 13). This expression was first noticed in Joshua 3:5. The sanctification mentioned here is not ceremonial, but spiritual. It deals with the commitment of the people to the covenant which they had with their God. It appears that lots were used in determining the guilty party. Notice the expression "the Lord taketh" (v. 14) and similar expressions throughout this section (cf. I Sam. 14:42; Jonah 1:7) which describe lot-casting elsewhere in Scripture. The first lot fell upon the tribe of Judah (v. 16); the second upon the clan Zerah (v. 17); the third upon the house of Zabdi (v. 17); the fourth and final lot fell upon the man Achan (v. 18). This event was followed by the confession of Achan (vv. 19-21). The sequence of Achan's temptation and sin, as described in verse 21, is instructive. His sin involved three crucial steps. (1) He saw; (2) he coveted, and (3) he took. This is not the first time that one has been led into sin by this means. Compare, for example, the experience of Eve in the Garden of Eden (Gen. 3:6), and the temptation of David (II Sam. 11:2-14). The objects taken by Achan included a "goodly Babylonish garment" (v. 7; Heb. "beautiful mantle of Shinar"). As previously noted, the presence of a garment from Shinar might indicate widespread trade contacts between Jericho and cities to the north. The stolen treasure also included two hundred shekels of silver, and a wedge (tongue or ingot) of gold. This wedge of gold was probably similar to the one unearthed at the city of Gezer by Macalister. It measured about ten inches, by one inch, by one-half inch. A similar wedge of gold is also mentioned in one of the Amarna letters.

2. *The Punishment of Sin* (7:22-26)

According to verse 24, not only Achan but his whole family was punished for the sin committed. We might assume from this act that the family had in some way taken part in this wicked deed. From a purely practical point of view, it is doubtful that Achan could have removed this number of objects and kept them concealed without some help from his family. The law of Deuteronomy 13:12-18 was probably in effect in this case. After he was stoned to death, they placed his body under a great heap of stones (v. 26) which appears to be a common method of burying infamous persons (cf. Josh. 8:29; II Sam. 18:17). The fact that all Israel (v. 24) participated in the punishment of Achan and his family seems to indicate that they had, indeed, sanctified themselves and were willing to deal with the sin problem. Once this had been cared for and the lesson had been learned, God was now ready to give victory to His people.

II. THE THRILL OF VICTORY (Josh. 8)

A. *The Battle Plan* (8:1-9)

Once again Jehovah encouraged Joshua not to be afraid nor be discouraged even though they had suffered defeat. He was commanded to take all the people of war and to go up to the city of Ai. As was the case with Jericho, the Lord promised to give the people and the city into his hands (v. 1). He was commanded to utterly destroy the city of Ai as he had done to the city of Jericho. However, the only difference was that they were permitted to take the spoil of that site; whereas, they were not permitted to do this in the conquest of Jericho (v. 2, cf. Josh. 6:18-21).

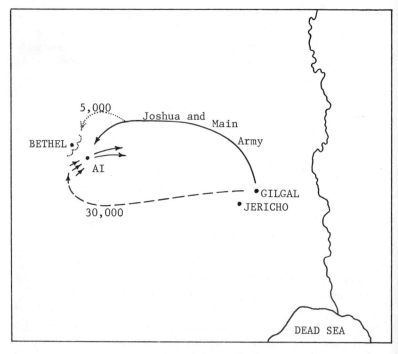

The Battle at Ai (Joshua 8)

The tactical maneuvers that were used in the capture of Ai are most interesting, but not without problems. For example, the numbers recorded in the verses that follow appear to be hopelessly confused; however, when they are studied carefully, they reveal an ingenious plan of attack and are very realistic. Joshua was commanded to select 30,000 men, and send them away by night to make the thirteen-mile journey to Ai, and then to lie in wait on the west side of the city (vv. 3-4). The next day, Joshua took the main army of Israel up to the north side of the city of Ai (v. 11). In addition to that move, another 5,000 were sent to lie in ambush between Bethel and Ai (v. 12). The map (page 56) will illustrate the battle plan as described in this chapter.

The 30,000 troops sent to the west side of Ai during the night were designed to be an attack force prepared to enter the city from that side. The main army of Joshua, encamped to the north, was to be used as a diversionary force to draw the armies of Ai out of the city, thereby leaving the city vulnerable to attack from the west (cf. vv. 13-17). The 5,000 troops, sent to the west side of Ai (v. 12), were deployed as a defensive measure designed to prevent the armies of Bethel from entering the battle or outflanking the 30,000 on the west side of the city of Ai.

B. *The Destruction of Ai* (8:10-29)

The battle plan worked to precision. The arrogant men of Ai were sure that they could again drive the Israelites down into the Jordan valley. However, when they fled down to the valley in pursuit of the fleeing Israelites, they turned back only to see their city in flames and smoke. The ambush of 30,000 men entered the city destroying it and killing all in their path. The 5,000 men encountered some resistance from Bethel and apparently were victorious there as well (cf. 8:17). Ultimately, the victory was complete. Over 12,000 men, women, and children were slain in this great battle (v. 25). In obedience to God's will, Joshua burned the city thus destroying it completely (v. 28, cf. v. 2). Following this, the king of Ai was slain and buried under a great heap of stones (v. 29).

C. *Archaeology and the Destruction of Ai*

The archaeological situation at the city of Ai is a very complex one as it regards the date of the conquest. Excavations were conducted at the site between 1933 and 1935 under the leadership of Madame Marquet-Krause. These excavations revealed that there was a major occupational gap between approximately 2200 B.C. and 1200 B.C. These data, of course, would not fit anyone's date of the Exodus. To shed additional light on the problem and to clarify the earlier excavations, Professor Joseph A. Calloway initiated excavations at the site in May of 1964. The results achieved that year and subsequent years have confirmed the presence of the occupational gap at this site. A number of solutions have been proposed with regard to this problem. There are those who suggest that the site should be located elsewhere in the vicinity. This view is difficult to maintain in the light of recent archaeological work by Dr. Calloway's teams. Many sites have now been eliminated in the vicinity of et-Tell. Some have suggested that the site suffers from major erosion such as was witnessed at Jericho, but this view seems to be unsatisfactory also. A very popular view is that the battle described in Joshua 8 really took place at Bethel and that the story of the battle was transferred to the ruins at Ai. Another writer has suggested that Ai was really a temporary fortress built near the site of Bethel. When this fortress was destroyed with its wall structures, nothing remained. At present, there is no easy or simple solution to the problem. We must await further investigation of both et-Tell and other sites in the central hill country in order to determine a solution to this difficulty.

D. *The Covenant Renewal at Mount Ebal* (8:30-35)

Following the great victory at Ai, the children of Israel marched northward to Mount Ebal, located about twenty miles north of et-Tell. Excavations conducted at the site of Shechem (Tell Balatah) indicate that there was a substantial occupation at this site about the time of the Israelites' arrival. Even though the site seems to have been fortified at this time, the Bible records no battle at this place. How were the Israelites able to move freely around Mount Gerizim and Mount Ebal without some confrontation from the inhabitants of Shechem? The answer to this problem might be found in several of the Amarna letters which were written about 1380 B.C. or shortly after the conquest period. These letters, written from the king of Jerusalem, and other cities, describe the surrender of the city of Shechem to the invading Habiru. The letters indicate, or at least imply, that the city surrendered without resistance. Is it not possible that the city of Shechem may have also succumbed to Israel in a similar manner? Some writers have suggested that perhaps some descendants of Jacob, who had left Egypt in small numbers before the oppression (cf. I Chron. 7:24), may have been at the site when Israel arrived there.

In any event, Israel moved successfully to the base of Mount Ebal, the mountain which is centrally situated in the land of Canaan. It rises to a height of 3,080 feet. Just to the south of it is the famous Mount Gerizim (2,849 feet). The mountains form a natural amphitheater in which the "cursings and blessings" could be pronounced and heard by those gathered at

Mount Gerizim (Joshua 8:33). Levant Photo Service

the site. Israel came to this site because Moses had specifically indicated that upon her entrance into the land, sacrifice and dedication should be made to God in this area (cf. Deut. 11: 26-30; 27:2-8). The first event was the establishment of an altar and sacrifices (v. 31). Following this, Joshua made a copy of the Law of Moses for all to read (vv. 32-34). The significance of this occasion cannot be overestimated. After a great victory, it was now Israel's responsibility to recognize the source of that victory, and again renew her covenant vows to Jehovah. Public readings of the law constituted a very important part of Israelite life and worship in many periods of her history (see Exod. 24:4, 7; II Kings 23:2; Neh. 8).

III. THE DANGER OF COMPLACENCY (Josh. 9)

After the great events at Mount Ebal, the children of Israel returned to the Jordan valley and their center of operations at Gilgal (cf. 9:6). It was at this place that the southern campaign would really begin. The chapter under consideration brings to our attention the fact that the kings of the Amorite city-states, who controlled the southern portions of Canaan, were desperately trying to form some kind of coalition in order to survive the invasion by the nation of Israel. Since Egypt showed no interest in the Palestinian cities at this time, they had no choice but to depend on one another for mutual defense (cf. vv. 1-2). The inhabitants of Gibeon, however, were not convinced that such a coalition would really be effective. They decided that a covenant agreement or a league would, in the long run, be more effective for them. Thus the Gibeonites, ingeniously, provide us with what might be termed an "Oscar winning performance" in deceiving the elders of Israel. The whole purpose of dressing up in old clothes, taking old sacks, and wearing old shoes was to convince the elders of Israel and Joshua that they had, indeed, been on the road for many days and had come from a "far country" (vv. 6, 9). The question is, "Why put on such a performance?" The answer to this question is to be found in two key texts: Deuteronomy 7:1-2 and 20: 10-15. These passages indicate that Israel was permitted to make peace with the cities that were far off, but not with the seven Canaanite nations living in close proximity to them. Somehow, the inhabitants of Gibeon found out about this legislation. The Gibeonites were very careful in their approach to the leaders of Israel. Beside the clothing, moldy food, and the proclamation that they were from a far country, they even omitted certain events in their discussion of Israel's recent history so as not to give themselves away. Notice that in verse ten they mention only the exodus from Egypt (v. 9) and the victories on the eastern side of the Jordan River (v. 10). There is no reference to the battle at Jericho or the destruction of the city of Ai. This, indeed, is appropriate, for if they had been on the road for many days — away from contact with cities, as evidenced by their moldy bread — then they should not have knowledge of the very recent battles. They proclaimed to the leaders of Israel that they were, in effect, willing to be "their servants" (vv. 9, 10). The use of this expression indicates the desire for a formal treaty or covenant. Such a treaty was drawn up by Joshua and the princes of Israel (9:15). This mistake which was made by Joshua was inexcusable in spite of the fact that the Gibeonites were shrewd in their deception of the elders of Israel. Verse 14 makes note of the fact that the Lord was not sought in the deliberations at hand. The treaty was made, and after three days, the Israelites knew that they had been deceived (v. 16). It is significant that the elders of Israel and Joshua refused to break that covenant even though they had been deceived. The Gibeonites were subjected to a state of servitude (v. 21), but the treaty remained intact. Some have questioned whether there was really any moral obligation on the part of Joshua and the elders to maintain that agreement in the light of the fact that they had been deceived. Others, on the basis of Leviticus 19:12, argue that they had a solemn and sacred responsibility to keep that oath since it was made in the name of the Lord God of Israel (v. 18). The forming of such agreements by the name of Jehovah was not a light matter and therefore they were morally responsible to maintain the agreement which they had made.

The practical lessons from this chapter should be obvious to the child of God. First of all, he should recognize that his enemy is cunning and deceitful. Secondly, he should trust every

Chapter 5

WHEN THE SUN STOOD STILL
(Joshua 10–12)

To make a formal oath or covenant in an ancient Near Eastern society was a very important — and in many respects a sacred — event. This was especially true in the case of Israel when, having been deceived, they made a covenant agreement with the Gibeonites in the name of Jehovah. The princes refused to break that oath, realizing that such a breach of agreement would bring wrath upon them (cf. Ezek. 17:12-19). Having made an agreement of peace between the Gibeonites and themselves, the Israelites were responsible not only for the keeping of peace, but for the protection of those people as they lived in servitude to Israel. The keeping of such a covenant agreement was not an easy task, as Chapter 10 demonstrates. In order to provide full protection for the Gibeonites, Joshua was drawn into battle against a major Amorite coalition from southern Canaan.

I. THE SOUTHERN CAMPAIGN (Chapter 10)

A. *The Plot against Gibeon* (10:1-6)

The surrender of the Gibeonites to Joshua and the elders of Israel was viewed as the beginning of a dangerous trend by Adoni-zedec, the king of Jerusalem (v. 1). Gibeon was a great city. In fact, the Bible describes it as one of the "royal cities," and a city that was greater than Ai having many mighty men (v. 2). If such an important city could surrender peacefully, this might pave the way for other cities in the vicinity of Jerusalem to surrender in like manner, or at least attempt to do so. This, of course, would be a serious threat to the security of Jerusalem. Adoni-zedec was probably a rather powerful king and an influential one in central Palestine. The Amarna Letters indicate that Jerusalem was the center of political activity in the fourteenth century B.C. and was always conscious of its own security. The name Adoni-zedec ("lord of righteousness") was probably a common Jebusite dynastic title rather than a personal name.

Gibeon (el-Jib) looking North (Joshua 9-10). Levant Photo Service

It is very similar to the name Melchizedek (Gen. 14:18) who was an earlier ruler in Jerusalem. The Jebusites (15:63), who controlled Jerusalem until the time of David when they were driven out, appear to be a racial mixture of Amorites, Hittites, and Hurrians (Ezek. 16:3). According to the Amarna Letters, written approximately 1375 B.C., there were only four main independent city-states in southern Palestine (Jerusalem, Shuwardata, Gezer, and Lachish). According to the Book of Joshua, however, there were approximately twenty-eight city-states having independent kings (12:9-16). This information appears to place Joshua's conquest prior to the writing of the Amarna Letters. The success of Israel brought about the end to many of the independent states thus leaving only a few self-sufficient political entities in southern Canaan, and also resulted in causing a good deal of confusion between those city-states.[20]

In order to punish the city of Gibeon for its deed, Adoni-zedec contacted other kings in southern Canaan located at Hebron,

[20]John Rea, *op. cit.*, p. 217.

Jarmuth, Lachish, and Eglon. The five kings responded posi-
tively to Adoni-zedec's plan and moved against Gibeon (v. 5).
When the Gibeonites received word of this plan, they immediately sent messengers to Joshua down at Gilgal (v. 6). They reminded Joshua of the covenant agreement that he had with the
city of Gibeon and requested protection in fulfillment of that
agreement.

B. *Joshua's March to Gibeon* (10:7-9)

Joshua recognized that he did have an obligation to protect
the city, and quickly responded to the plea of the Gibeonites.
It is clear from verse 8 that all of this was, indeed, in accordance
with the Lord's will, for He had given assurance that victory
would be theirs. Joshua gathered his forces together, and during
that evening they began their march to Gilgal — a journey of
approximately twenty-five miles. Such a journey must have been
very tiring to the soldiers even though they traveled in the
evening. It is apparent that Jehovah would have to help them
if they were to realize the victory promised to them.

C. *The Defeat of the Amorite Coalition* (10:10-27)

1. *The Miracle of Hailstones* (10:10-11)

The battle that is described in the verses that follow is one of
the most unusual in Israel's history. In fact, it is one of the most
unusual in all recorded history. When the Israelites first confronted the Amorite coalition, the Lord aided their battle plan
by discomfiting the enemy. This was accomplished by providing a hailstorm (v. 11). There is no other way to explain this
event than to regard it as a miracle, for it appears that the
hailstones affected only the enemy and not Israel. It is not
characteristic of a purely natural hailstorm to make such a
selection! The events described in verses 10 and 11 most likely
took place in very early morning. As the day wore on, it became
evident to Joshua that they would not be able to complete the
battle and gain victory. He also realized that if the enemy were
to have the benefit of darkness and rest, it would be most
difficult for Israel to confront them again. His troops were tired,

but everything at this point was in his favor. The enemy was scattered and frustrated as a result of the hailstorm. He wanted to capitalize on this situation, thus, in verse 12, he appeared before the Lord and brought to the Lord a most unusual request.

2. *The Miracle of Extended Light* (10:12-27)

This portion of Scripture has long been subjected to speculative ideas and interpretations because of the nature of the events herein described. It will not be our purpose to present an exhaustive treatment of the many views offered, but rather a brief summary and evaluation of some of them, followed by the writer's view of this passage.

There are three basic interpretations of the long day of Joshua. (a) *The total eclipse view.* The essence of this view is that God brought darkness rather than light on this occasion. The advocates for this view contend that God actually caused the sun and the moon to stop shining. This was accomplished by the use of clouds, a hailstorm, or perhaps an eclipse of the sun. The arguments for this view are generally based on the Hebrew word *dom*, which usually means "to be silent." It can also have as a secondary meaning, however, the idea of "to cease" or "to desist." The latter translation is suggested by R. D. Wilson, who gave this view prominence in an article written some years ago in *Princeton Theological Review*.[21] It is argued that if the sun could be shaded, it would provide relief for the weary armies of Joshua. While this approach seems plausible at first, careful consideration indicates that it does not fulfill the requirements of the passage. If the sun were to cease shining, thereby providing rest and refreshment for Joshua's soldiers, would this not also be the case for the enemy? In the second place, we might observe that the Scripture describes this as a very unique day. Notice the words of verse 14: "And there was no day like that before it or after it." This seems to be a rather extravagant statement if the event was merely the shading or the eclipsing

---

[21]R. D. Wilson, "What Does 'The Sun Stood Still' Mean?" *Princeton Theological Review* Vol. 16, 1918.

of the sun. The sun has been darkened before, and we have had many eclipses subsequent to that period of history. The statement, therefore, seems to indicate a day which has no parallel in history. (b) *The Poetic interpretation.* According to this view, the account of the battle is nothing more than poetic imagery and should not be taken literally. It is argued that the ideas expressed in these verses were purely subjective, i.e., that it only *seemed* like the sun stood still because of the heat of the battle. It is true that verse 13 is a quotation from the book of Jasher and that it is indeed in poetic structure. However, it is not uncommon for literal battles and attending events to be described in poetic language (cf. Judg. 4-5).[22] (c) *The prolongation of light interpretation.* This view, by and large the most popular view of conservative commentators, is that which understands the passage literally. In other words, it assumes that there was an actual extension of light for about a whole day, thereby permitting Joshua to complete the battle. While there is wide agreement among conservative scholars on this general position, there is a great divergence of opinion relative to the method by which this prolongation of light was accomplished.

The following are some representative views on this problem: (1) *The slowing of the earth's rotation.* Many commentators feel that the simplest solution to the extension of light suggested in this chapter is to propose a slowing down of the earth's rotation. There is no question that God was fully capable of such a miracle. At this point, the question is, "Would such a miracle be performed merely to provide assistance to the armies fighting in the area of Beth-horon?" (2) *A comet came near the earth.* Immanuel Velikovsky suggests that the reason the earth's rotation was slowed down was due to the appearance of a comet near the earth, thus exerting gravitational pull on it and disrupting its normal movement. The tail of this comet, he claims, provided the "stones" that dispersed the enemy.[23]

---

[22]For further discussion of this view, see F. R. Fay, *Joshua, Commentary on the Holy Scriptures,* Trans. Philip Schaff (Grand Rapids: Zondervan Publishing House, n.d.), p. 96 ff.

[23]Immanuel Velikovsky, *Worlds in Collison* (New York: Macmillan, 1950), pp. 43-44.

This view is typical of those approaches to Scriptures which would attempt to explain miracles by means of natural phenomena or catastrophes. It is very doubtful that a comet with whatever magnetic field it might contain would ever effect the movement of the earth with its great mass, and, of course, it is highly questionable that stones falling from the tail of a comet would strike the enemy and not harm Israel. The most obvious objection to this view is that there is no archaeological or geological evidence of such an event in Palestine. (3) *The tilting of the earth*. George Williams in *The Student's Commentary* suggests that the means that God used to extend light was to tilt the earth on its axis thus causing the sun to remain above the horizon as it does, for example, in Norway during the summer.[24] Again, this view creates more problems than it solves. If the earth were tilted in this manner, it would be observed in the position of the sun. Also, such tilting would create radical changes in climate. This view, like that of slowing the earth's rotation, assumes that the miracle performed was universal in scope. (4) *The principle of jet propulsion*. In the *Sunday School Times* of August 15, 1942, Hawley O. Taylor proposed that the earth's rotation was indeed slowed down. In order to provide a mechanism for this event, he made the suggestion that a number of volcanic explosions took place, all, of course, facing the east, thus providing a counter-thrust causing the crust of the earth to slow down in rotation. The liquid interior of the earth, however, continued to rotate in its normal pattern. After a period of time the outside crust of the earth resumed rotation along with the inside. This view really does not deserve serious scientific consideration. In the first place, it is impossible that volcanos could ever produce this kind of thrust, and, of course, this view assumes that all the volcanos would be aimed in a certain direction. This would require an immense miracle. The earth has a mass of about six trillion tons and at the equator is moving about a thousand miles an hour. No series of volcanic thrusts could ever produce enough velocity to slow down the rotation of the earth, and even if such volcanos did erupt, it would

---

[24]George Williams, *The Student's Commentary on the Holy Scriptures* (London: Oliphants Ltd, 1949), p. 114.

bring about mass destruction over large areas of the earth. Views like this do little to help the cause of serious Biblical interpretation.

(5) *The refraction or extension of the sun's rays on a local level.* The best solution to this problem is to regard it as a local miracle performed by God. It is very doubtful that the Lord would have performed a universal miracle involving the whole earth in its relationship to the sun merely to extend light for a relatively brief period in the area of Gibeon. There is an economy of the exercise of God's miraculous power both in the Old and the New Testaments, and in the light of this, a universal miracle involving the whole earth seems rather doubtful. We might note at this point that if such a universal miracle were performed, it would be one of the greatest miracles in Scripture, superseding that of the dividing of the Red Sea or the crossing of the Jordan River. However, there is only one other reference to this event in Scripture, found in Habakkuk 3:11. Furthermore, there was another time when the sun's relationship to the earth was altered in some way. This event, recorded in II Kings 20:10-11, required the shadow on the sundial to go back ten degrees. If we regard this as a literal, universal miracle, it would mean that God would not only have had to slow down the rotation of the earth, but reverse it for the mere purpose of changing the shadow on the sundial of Hezekiah. It is extremely doubtful that such a miracle was performed on that occasion. In fact, the parallel passage found in II Chronicles 32:24-31 seems to imply that it was a local miracle. Verse 24 of this passage indicates that God gave a special sign to Hezekiah. That sign was evidently witnessed only in Palestine, for verse 31 records the fact that ambassadors from Babylon were sent down to Hezekiah to "inquire of the wonder that was done *in the land.*" If the miracle performed in the days of Hezekiah was universal, there would be little need for ambassadors to come all the way from Babylon to inquire of the miracle. The text seems to indicate that this miracle occurred only in the Jerusalem area (cf. v. 31 "in the land"), was witnessed — or word was passed around Jerusalem concerning the event — and it ultimately reached the city of Babylon. The astronomers there decided to investigate the matter, thus sending representatives

down to Jerusalem. If the miracle of the sundial was local, then we might assume that the miracle performed for Joshua was also local in scope and did not involve other countries of the world. Somewhat parallel to this event would be the plague of darkness in Egypt (Exod. 10:21-23). There God supernaturally darkened only portions of the land while there was light in the areas occupied by Israel. No one seriously proposes that God darkened the whole earth for the purpose of punishing the people in Egypt. This view is also consistent with the many statements of Scripture which relate to the faithfulness of God's laws regarding day and night (cf. Gen. 1; 8:22; Jer. 33:20 ff.).

The precise method which God used to extend light is really not important at this point. It is clear from Scripture that the extension of light was sufficient to give Joshua and the children of Israel the upper hand in the battle. The kings of the Amorites were forced to flee to the northwest by way of Beth-horon to the Shephelah. From there they continued southwestward along the valleys toward Azekah and finally to Makkedah which was about twenty miles from Gibeon. On the next day the kings were discovered in a cave near Makkedah. They were taken from the cave and ceremonially the officers of Joshua were commanded to put their feet upon the necks of these kings (10:16-20). Such an act was a symbol of the complete subjugation of the defeated enemy. Many times such acts are pictured on monuments of Egyptian and Assyrian kings (cf. I Kings 5:3; Ps. 8:6; 18:38 ff.; Isa. 49:23). Following this the men were slain and their bodies hanged on trees (v. 26, cf. Deut. 21:22; Num. 25:4).

D. The Conquest of Southern Palestine (10:28-43)

1. The Nature of the Campaign

The battle of Beth-horon was the first step in the southern campaign. The battle continued in days following through Makkedah (v. 28), Libnah (v. 29), Lachish (v. 31) Eglon (v. 34), Hebron (v. 36), and Debir (v. 38). Joshua, at this stage of the campaign, did not seem to be interested in completely destroying each one of the sites, or occupying that site. The nature of his campaign took the form of lightning-like raids against the

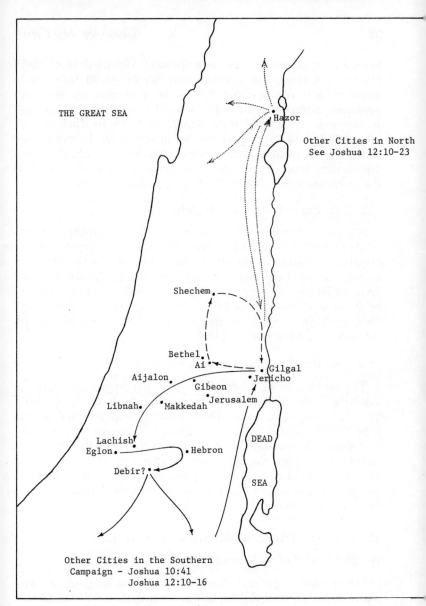

THE GREAT SEA

Hazor

Other Cities in North
See Joshua 12:10-23

Shechem

Bethel
Ai

Aijalon

Gibeon

Libnah

Makkedah

Jerusalem

Gilgal

Jericho

Lachish

Eglon

Hebron

Debir?

DEAD

SEA

Other Cities in the Southern
Campaign - Joshua 10:41
Joshua 12:10-16

The Campaigns of Joshua

key military centers in southern Canaan. The purpose of these raids was to destroy the military capacity of the important city-states of this area and not necessarily to occupy the sites immediately after the battle. There is evidence that many of the battles were not even fought within the cities themselves (10:33; 12:12; 16:10. It would not be practical for Joshua to lay siege to many of these well-fortified cities for such a siege would take a long time. Furthermore, it would not really accomplish the purpose of the campaign at this period.

2. *The Purpose of the Campaign*

It appears that the purpose of the southern campaign was essentially twofold: (a) to destroy the military capacity of the important city-states, and (b) to strike fear and bring confusion among the other city-states in southern Canaan. There does not seem to be any attempt to occupy or to take complete control of the area, or even to establish garrisons in conquered territory. In fact, there is evidence that several of the sites had to be retaken at a later period (15:13-17).

3. *The Results of the Campaign*

The latter part of Chapter 10 gives the impression that the campaign was indeed quite successful. In a relatively brief period of time, Joshua was able to secure at least minimal control over the Shephelah and the southern hill country as far south as Lachish. It would now be the responsibility of the individual tribes to conquer the remaining sections of the territory as helped by the Lord. Following the conquest of this territory, Joshua and the armies of Israel returned to the Jordan valley to their encampment at Gilgal (v. 43).

II. THE NORTHERN CAMPAIGN (Chapter 11)

A. *The Coalition of Northern City-States* (11:1-5)

When word of Joshua's success reached the kings of the city-states in the areas of Galilee and westward, they decided to take immediate steps to protect their own territory. The leader of this coalition was Jabin, king of Hazor (v. 1). The name Jabin should be regarded as a dynastic title rather than a personal name (cf. Judg. 4:2; Ps. 83:9). The city of Hazor was at this time the head of all the kingdoms in the north (v. 10). It is understandable why Jabin, therefore, would assume leadership in this matter. The coalition army that was formed was a rather impressive one. The main strike force included horses and chariots in great numbers (vv. 4-5).

B. *The Destruction of Hazor* (11:6-23)

As the armies began to mass in great numbers in the northern

Hazor (Tell el-Kedah), the head of the city-states in the North (Joshua 11:10). Matson Photo Service

plains of Palestine, the Lord again appeared to Joshua and comforted him, promising that victory would be given to him again by the Lord's help (v. 6). Joshua was given specific battle instructions by the Lord on this occasion and these included the houghing of the enemies' horses as well as burning their chariots (v. 6). The word "hough" would be better translated "hamstring." The purpose of this act was to prevent Israel from gathering to themselves great military weapons and a large chariot force, for in time they would depend on these things rather than on their God (cf. Deut. 17:16; Ps. 20:7; Isa. 31:1). As in times past, God fulfilled His promise to the people of Israel. A great victory was given to the armies of Israel allowing them to destroy their enemy, burn the chariots and take the city of Hazor (vv. 9-14). When the city was conquered, it was burned with fire. It, evidently, was the only city so treated in the northern campaign (cf. v. 13). This was no small victory, for archaeology has demonstrated that Hazor was indeed a great city. In the Late Bronze Age it covered an area of about 170 acres, supporting a population of anywhere from thirty to forty thousand people. There is a problem in connection with the archaeological data and Joshua's campaign. According to recent discoveries, the occupation of Hazor continued down through the thirteenth century without apparent major interruption. The answer to this problem might be found in the nature of the destruction and the immediate reoccupation of the site. The site was indeed burned according to Scripture, but if the Canaanites immediately reoccupied it and rebuilt it, as the fourth chapter of Judges seems to indicate, we may have little or no evidence of Joshua's destruction of the city.

The northern campaign of Joshua involved more than the city of Hazor. It included many of the important city-states and smaller towns in the northern hills of Galilee and cities in the lowland (cf. vv. 16-18). The Lord played an important role not only in giving Israel victory but in caring for the attitude of the enemy. According to verse 20, the Lord hardened the hearts of the enemy in order that they would not attempt to make peace with Israel but would face them in battle. This is reminiscent of God's activity with regard to Pharaoh in Egypt (cf. Exod. 4:21; 7:13 ff.; 9:12; 14:17; also Isa. 6:10; John 12:40).

The success of Joshua's campaigns is further illustrated in verses 21-23. The Anakim mentioned in these verses were the gigantic sons of Anak who terrified the spies some forty years before (Num. 13:28, 33; Deut. 9:2). These people were now reduced to a mere remnant living in southwestern Palestine (v. 22). It is significant that the area in which they remained was the very gateway back to Egypt.

III. THE LIST OF DEFEATED KINGS (Chapter 12)

This chapter summarizes the great victories on both the east side of the Jordan and the west side. Verses 1-6 of this chapter describe the conquest of the territories of Sihon and Og under the leadership of Moses. The cities of the west side are listed in verses 7-24. The thirty-one kings defeated by Joshua were local kings having limited power. Verses 9-16 list the kings of southern Canaan, while verses 17-24 make note of the defeated kings in northern Canaan. The list is important because it points out the significant military sites during Joshua's day. Many of the same names appear in the Amarna Letters, thus confirming the historicity of our text.

Two important truths stand out in these three chapters which are worthy of special consideration. (1) *The power of God.* When the battle raged in the area of Beth-horon, and Joshua desperately needed additional light, God miraculously provided that light. In the eleventh chapter the power of God was evident in giving victory to Israel in spite of the fact that they were outnumbered and did not have the sophisticated military equipment possessed by the Canaanites. The power of God was also exhibited in 11:20, when He prepared the hearts of the enemy so that they might be defeated in the fulfillment of His own purpose. (2) *The faith of Joshua.* One cannot help but take note of the attitude and unqualified obedience of the man Joshua. He acted not on the basis of the military strength of Israel or on his own genius in the area of tactical maneuvers, but on the promises of God alone. He did not require confirmations or signs, nor did he ask for an extension of time or additional arms. The life of Joshua and the events recorded in these chapters have a very practical bearing upon our own present-

Chapter 6

FIRST STEPS IN SETTLEMENT
(Joshua 13—24)

The significant military victories recorded in the first twelve chapters of the Book of Joshua were only first steps in the settlement of the land. Chapters 13—24 describe the assignment of land made to various tribes in considerable geographical detail. According to the words of Jacob (Gen. 49) and Moses (Deut. 33), the tribes were to anticipate a blessing in the land. The children of Israel at this particular time occupied very little of the land of Canaan. However, Joshua had been successful in removing the significant military threats to Israel's existence. It would now be the responsibility of the tribes to conquer and to colonize their designated territories. The chapters that follow describe the method and the result of land division as assigned to the various tribes. It should be kept in mind that the lists were drawn up before the tribes actually settled the territories and therefore are in some respects idealistic. In reality, most of the tribes did not conquer or control all of their alloted territories (cf. Josh. 15:63; 16:10; 17:12-16; 19:47).

I. DIVIDING THE LAND (13:1—21:45)

A. *The Method of Division* (13:1—14:5)

According to 14:1, three parties were involved in the division of the land: Eleazar the priest, Joshua, and the heads of the fathers of the tribes. The casting of lots before the Lord was the divinely appointed method by which each tribe would receive its share of land (cf. 13:6; 14:2; 18:6).[25] The principal division of territory was between the tribes of Judah and Joseph; the other allotments of land would be contingent upon the area given to these tribes. The allotment of certain territories was not a haphazard procedure. According to 18:4-9, a special group of men was set aside to study the land and to designate border

---

[25]Compare Numbers 26:52 ff.; 33:54; 34:13.

areas. The size of a tribe was also a factor in the assignment of
special territories (cf. Num. 26:51-56; 33:54). Various land-
marks were used in the delineation of borders. According to
Chapter 15, the seas (vv. 2, 4), the rivers (v. 4), the mountains
(vv. 8, 10), the desert (v. 1), and towns (v. 21 ff.) were all
border indicators. This method of boundary definition is paralleled in a document by Suppiluliuma (a Hittite king of the
fourteenth century B.C.), to Niqmadu of Ugarit, Ras Shamra.[26]

Joshua at this time was old and advancing in years (13:1).
In spite of his age, however, it was imperative that he continue
his leadership over the nation and guide in the allotment of
tribal territories. The Lord had instructed him that he was not
only to achieve military victory in the land, but was to assume
leadership in the division of the inheritance in the land (cf. 1:6).

When the Lord spoke to Joshua regarding his responsibility
in the land division, mention was made of the Philistines (13:
2-3). This is the only time the Philistines are mentioned in the
Book of Joshua. According to 11:22, it was the Anakim who in-
habited Gaza, Gath, and Ashdod. Since the Philistines were not
listed among the inhabitants of the land (cf. 12:8), it is apparant
that they were still confined to the coastal area of the Negeb
(cf. Exod. 13:17). This was the same area in which they appeared during the Patriarchal Age (cf. Gen. 21:32; 26:1). John
Rea suggests, "In the light of the foregoing evidence, Joshua
13:3 is perhaps an early scribal notation to inform us that the do-
main of the five Philistine lords (seren, Judges 16:5; I Sam. 5:8)
in Joshua's day still belonged to the Canaanites."[27]

The remaining part of Chapter 13 enumerates the tribal allotments with regard to the territory of Transjordan. Reuben
(13:5-23) was given the territory which was previously occupied
by Moab, just to the east of the Dead Sea. The tribe of Gad
(13:24-28) was given territory north of the Arnon River in the
original land of Gilead. The territory east of the Sea of Galilee
was assigned to one-half the tribe of Manasseh (13:29-33).
The other half of the tribe had elected to settle on the west
side of the Jordan with the remaining tribes.

---

[26]See Claude Schaefer, *Les Palais Royal d'Ugarit* IV, 10-18.

[27]John Rea, "Joshua," *The Wycliffe Bible Commentary*, p. 222.

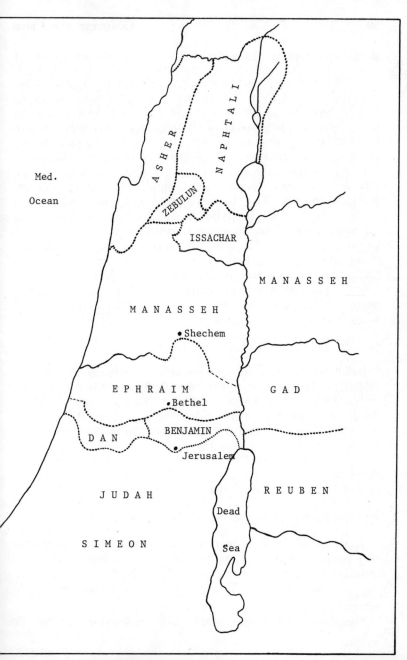

The Tribal Allotments

B. *Caleb's Portion* (14:6-15)

Caleb is one of the outstanding characters in the Joshua narratives. He was a man of faith and courage (cf. Num. 13:30; 14:6). According to Joshua 14:14, he "wholly followed the Lord God of Israel." Because of his faithfulness to his God, and his faithfulness to Joshua in the difficult years of conquest, he was given a special portion of land in the area of Hebron, earlier known as Kirjath-arba (Josh. 14:15). Caleb's statement of age, recorded in Joshua 14:10, is most significant in evaluating the Joshua narratives. The statement gives us a clue to the length of the actual conquest of the land. According to this verse, the main thrust of the conquest would have taken seven years. Caleb pointed out that forty-five years had passed since the giving of the promise to him. That promise was given to him thirty-eight years before the crossing of the Jordan (cf. Num. 14:24). The actual time of conquest was therefore about seven years. According to this verse, Caleb was about forty years old when Moses sent him out as a spy.[28]

C. *The Portion of Judah* (15:1-63)

Judah was the first tribe to receive an inheritance on the west side of the Jordan River. Because of the size of Judah, a considerable portion of land was given to it. This allotment included the territory south of a line extending west from the northern tip of the Dead Sea, bounded on the west by the Mediterranean, on the south by a line from the southern end of the Dead Sea to the River of Egypt (Wadi el-Arish), and on the east by the Dead Sea. Caleb's territory was included in the tribal territory of Judah, as was that of the Simeonites (19:1-9).

D. *The Portion of the Joseph Tribes* (16:1—17:18)

The tribe of Ephraim was located immediately north of Dan and Benjamin (cf. map, page 79). The borders of Ephraim included the Jordan River on the east, the Mediterranean on the west, and the Kanah Valley and eastward on the north. Just

---

[28]Josephus gives the duration of the conquest as five years, *Ant.* V: 1:19.

north of Ephraim was the territory of the tribe of Manasseh. The Mediterranean on the west, the Jordan on the east, and the valley of Jezreel on the north constituted the basic borders of the tribe of Manasseh. The tribe of Ephraim, therefore, controlled part of the central hill country, and the tribe of Manasseh controlled the remaining central hill country up to the valley of Jezreel. The Scripture gives us important insights to the success of these tribes in actually occupying their territories. For example, in 16:10, we are informed that the Ephraimites were incapable of driving out the inhabitants of Gezar. In fact, the city of Gezer did not come under full Israelite control until the day of Solomon (cf. I Kings 9:16). This text also provides information with regard to the materialistic attitude of the Ephraimites, for rather than conquering and driving out the Canaanites in their territory, they put them under "tribute," thereby gaining additional wealth. A similar description is given of the efforts of Manasseh in 17:12, 13. They, too, were incapable of complete victory and colonization; and like Ephraim, rather than destroying the Canaanites, they put them to tribute (cf. Judg. 1:28). This policy of coalition had disastrous effects in the years that followed.

E. *The Portions of the Remaining Seven Tribes* (18:1—19:51)

The tribal allotments up to this point were conducted in the central camp area at Gilgal. According to 18:1, the center of attention then shifted to Shiloh, which for three hundred years was the center of Israelite political and religious activity. Benjamin was given the territory between Ephraim and Judah. His territory was not very large, but centrally located and therefore constituted an important section of land.

North of the valley of Jezreel four more tribes received territory. Zebulun (19:10-16) was given territory north of Mt. Carmel, east of the Mediterranean, and south of the upper Galilean hills. It reached to the east almost to the Sea of Chinneroth. Just south of it, but north of the tribe of Manasseh, was the territory given to Issachar (19:17-23). Asher, on the other hand, settled along the Mediterranean coast, north of the tribe of Zebulun, and west of Naphtali. The Phoenicians were located

Site of Shiloh showing excavation dump to the left in the distance
Matson Photo Service

on the northern borders of its territory (cf. 19:24-31). The territory of Naphtali is delineated in 19:32-39. It was located to the east of Asher and north of Zebulun (see map, page 79). The final allotment came to the tribe of Dan (19:40-48). The Danites were assigned a parcel of land west of Ephraim and along the Mediterranean coast. The Amorites, who settled portions of the Philistine plain (Judg. 1:34), drove the Danites out of the plains and into the hills. This led to a migration of part of the tribe of Dan northward to Leshem near the northern part of Naphtali (cf. Judg. 17, 18). Joshua waited until all territories had been given to the tribes, and at that time he received an inheritance. This portion of land was located in the mountainous district of Ephraim which was his tribe (Josh. 19:49-51).

F. *The Cities of Refuge* (20:1-9)

Because of the widespread practice of blood revenge, God promised a place where the unintentional manslayer might flee (Exod. 21:13). The word "refuge" comes from the Hebrew *qālaṭ* which means "to contract, to draw, to take in, or to receive." The full expression in the Hebrew text is *'ārê hamiqlāṭ.* All of the cities listed in this chapter were Levitical cities, and therefore in a special sense provided divine protection for the unwitting manslayer (cf. Num. 35:9-34; Deut. 4:41ff.; 19:1-13). The Old Testament makes a clear distinction between premeditated murder and unintentional manslaughter (cf. Num. 35:11-16). The taking of a human life in the Old Testament period was viewed as a serious matter, especially in the light of man's relationship to God (cf. Gen. 9:6, see also Exod. 21:12, 14). Where murder had been committed, it was the responsibility of the nearest kinsman or the "avenger of blood" (Heb. *go'ēl hadām*) to punish the guilty party (Deut. 19:12). For the man who unintentionally killed another, there was divine protection and a trial. He was permitted to flee to one of the six cities. There he would be presented at the gate before the ancient law court (cf. Deut. 21:19; 22:15). Later he was brought to stand trial before the congregation of the community nearest the scene of the crime. If he was deemed innocent of premeditated murder, he was returned to the city of refuge until the death of the high priest. Then he could return to his home.[29] The six cities which were set aside for such asylum were located on both the east and the west sides of the Jordan River. The three on the west side were Kedesh in Galilee, and Shechem in the mountains of Ephraim, and Hebron in the mountains of Judah. The three on the east side, described in verse 8, were Bezer in the south, Ramoth in the area of Gilead, and Golan in the territory of Bashan.

G. *The Levitical Cities* (Josh. 21:1-45)

The Levites were not given any specific allotments of territory. It was God's purpose that they should be scattered throughout the tribes of Israel to act as a spiritual influence and to teach the law (cf. Josh. 13:33; 14:3; 18:7; Deut. 18:1-2). When the leaders of the Levites appeared before Eleazar and Joshua, they requested that their assignment of cities be carried out (21:1 ff.). This was not an unjustified request. God had promised that they would be cared for (Num. 35:1-2). The Levites were assigned forty-eight cities including the pasture lands or "suburbs" around them (Josh. 21:41).

II. PREPARING FOR SETTLEMENT (JOSH. 22–24)

A. *The Jordan Altar* (22:1-34)

After the initial conquest of the land and the allotment of territories to the various tribes, Joshua called the Reubenites, the Gadites and the half tribe of Manasseh together. On this occasion, he commended them for their faithfulness to him throughout the difficult years of conquest (22:2; cf. 1:17). Moses originally gave them permission to settle the territory of Transjordan provided that they would join their brethren in the conquest of Canaan (Num. 32:1-42). The two-and-one-half tribes fulfilled this responsibility and as a consequence were praised by Joshua. While their military commitments had been fulfilled Joshua reminded them that they had spiritul commitments which

---

[29]John Rea, "Joshua," p. 227.

would continue. These are expressed in verse 5 of this chapter. The six infinitives are employed to emphasize their responsibility to the Word of God and to His will. The admonitions given were very important in the light of the fact that these tribes would be separated from their brothers. The Jordan Valley was indeed a significant barrier to continuous contact with the tribes located in Canaan. As a result of successful conquest and faithfulness in responding to military needs, the two-and-one-half tribes returned with silver, gold, cattle, bronze, and iron (v. 8).

The events in this chapter raise an important question as to the right of the two-and-one-half tribes to settle the area of Transjordan. Many have argued that their presence in Transjordan was in opposition to the will of God. They argue that the reason for settlement on the east side of the Jordan was purely selfish. It is their feeling that the events recorded in Numbers 32 indicate the self-centered interest of the two-and-one-half tribes. Moses merely accommodated himself to their wishes. However, one does not gain this impression with a careful study of Joshua 22 or related portions. It appears in the first place, that the eastern boundary of the Promised Land was not the Jordan Valley, but the mountain range of Gilead. Secondly, Joshua blessed the tribes and indicated that they indeed did have a right to settlement in Transjordan. Thirdly, the fact that God delivered the land of Sihon and Og to Israel seems to imply that someone was to possess it (Josh. 24:8).

Following the counsels of Joshua, the two-and-one-half tribes proceeded to make their way back across the Jordan to their families and homeland. On the way, they erected an altar on the west bank of the Jordan River (cf. v. 10). When the other tribes saw this altar, they were convinced that the eastern tribes were attempting to set up an altar in opposition to the one at Shiloh. They gathered themselves together at Shiloh and prepared for war (v. 12). Phinehas, the son of Eleazar the priest, stepped in and offered to arbitrate in order to ascertain the nature of the case (vv. 13 ff.). In verses 16 ff., the charge against the two-and-one-half tribes takes the form of three kinds of sin. In verse 16, reference is made to a trespass (Heb. *ma'al*). The word for trespass as used in this verse is the same one employed in 7:1, in connection with the sin of Achan. The sin of the two-and-one-half tribes was also likened to the "iniquity of Peor" (v. 17). The iniquity of Peor had as an essential element idolatry and open disobedience to God's will with regard to worship (cf. Num. 25). Finally, their sin is described as an act of rebellion (vv. 18-19).

The defense of the two-and-one-half tribes is recorded in verses 21-29. Their response was that of innocence to the charges placed against them. Their principal concern was that their children would have equal rights to worship and movement throughout the land on the west side of the Jordan. They saw the Jordan Valley as a natural barrier to continued fellowship between the tribes. In order to care for the possibility of this problem arising in the future, they felt that a ceremonial altar should be erected as a sign of their right to worship in Shiloh. This altar, according to them, was not designed for sacrifice but merely as a witness (Heb. *'ēḏ*) between them and the future generations living on the west banks of the Jordan (vv. 26-27). It is entirely possible that the altar which was erected was patterned after the one at Shiloh and perhaps this is the reason that the other tribes reacted as they did. In verse 28, reference is made to the "pattern of the altar of Jehovah." The Hebrew word for "pattern" is *taḇnîṯ* which literally means a "form, model, replica, or pattern." This might mean that their altar was patterned after the one at Shiloh and therefore, at least from outward appearance, would be designed for sacrifice. When the explanation was given, Phinehas and the princes were satisfied that the motives of the two-and-one-half tribes were indeed pure.

Even though a war was averted at this time, it became clear that there would be a problem of unity between the tribes settled on the east side of the Jordan and those in Canaan. Strictly speaking, the action of the two-and-one-half tribes was both needless and presumptuous. According to the law, all Israelite males were to appear before the Lord at the tabernacle three times a year (Exod. 23:17). God had not given instructions for the building of any other monument. Furthermore, it was God's plan that through faithful worship at Shiloh, all the tribes would remain together in unity. The action taken by the two-and-one-half tribes was merely the first in a series of independent

acts on the part of various tribes which would lead to later fragmentation of the tribes of Israel. Building other altars was, in
fact, a departure from God's plan for centralized worship. The
unifying factor in ancient Israel was not her culture, architecture,
economy, or even military objectives. The long-range unifying
factor was her worship of Jehovah. When the central sanctuary
was abandoned as the true place of worship, the tribes then
developed independent sanctuaries, thus alienating themselves
from other tribes and weakening their military potential. The
effects of this trend are fully seen in the period of the Judges.

B. *The Last Words of Joshua* (23–24)

1. *Principles for Successful Occupation of the Land* (23:1-16)

Near the end of Joshua's life, he appeared before the tribes
with final warnings with regard to God's will for them in the
land. He was at this time rather old. We would assume that
he was between the age of 100 and 110 years (23:1, cf. 24:
29). Joshua reminded them that their successful conquest of
the land was dependent upon God's work in their behalf. They
were to recognize that successful occupation and colonization
of the land would require no less. Two principal requirements
were laid before Israel with regard to future occupation of their
territory. The first was unqualified obedience to the Word of
God (vv. 1-6). As in the first chapter of this book, so we are
again reminded of the authority of the written Word of God.
The principles for godly activity were not to be found in the
land of Canaan, but were clearly revealed in the book of the
law of Moses (v. 6). The second qualification for prosperity of
the land involved separation (vv. 7-16). That separation had
both a negative and a positive aspect. They were to be separated
from the gods of the land (v. 7, cf. Exod. 23:13; Deut. 12:3).
They were also to remain separate from the peoples of the
nations (v. 7). The positive aspect of their separation is described in the eighth verse. They were separated not only from
the world about them but *unto* their God.

Joshua did not merely settle for a series of public admonitions
in order to guide Israel after his death. The twenty-fourth
chapter describes a formal covenant renewal enacted at the

site of Shechem for the purpose of getting a binding commitment on the part of the people of Israel to the written Word of God. In the light of the events of Joshua 8, it is significant that this gathering should be called to the site of Shechem. Modern critical scholars argue that this chapter records the real beginning of the "nation" of Israel. They refer to Israel as here forming an amphictyony — an association of neighboring tribes around a common religious center. As one writer puts it, "The ceremony represents the inauguration of a twelve-tribe confederacy . . ."[30] Such a theory does not deserve detailed refutation, for at its basis is a denial of all historicity to Biblical narratives and in many cases ignores positive archaeological evidence supporting the claims of Scripture. Joshua 23:16 indicates that a formal covenant *was already in existence.* This covenant, of course, was established at Sinai shortly after the exodus from Egypt. Therefore, what we have in Chapter 24 is a *covenant renewal,* not the establishment of a new covenant.

The literary form of Chapter 24 is parallel to the well-known suzerainty treaties of the Middle East dating from this period of time. In such a treaty, a monarch obligated his vassals to serve him in faithfulness and obedience. Such treaties are common in the international agreements between the Hittite empire and its vassal states (1450-1200 B.C.).[31] Verses 1 and 2 constitute the preamble to the covenant renewal. In it we have the identification of the God of Israel and the parties involved in the treaty agreement. Verses 2-13 describe the historical prologue; that is, the provision made by the king for his people. In this section Joshua reviewed God's blessing upon His nation from the time that Abraham was called from the land of Mesopotamia up until their conquest of the land of Canaan. In every case, God provided for the military and economic needs of Israel.

Verse 12 of this section graphically describes the Lord's sending of a "hornet" before them. This expression has given rise

---

[30]Berhard W. Anderson, "The Place of Shechem in the Bible," *The Biblical Archaeologist,* Vol. 20, No. 1 (Feb., 1957), p. 14.

[31]See George E. Mendenhall, *Law and Covenant in Israel and the Near East* (Pittsburgh: The Biblical Colloquium, 1955).

to considerable speculation as to what the "hornet" must have been. Two principal views have emerged. First, John Garstang understood it as a veiled reference to the Egyptian armies that had defeated the Hyksos and other peoples in Palestine shortly before the conquest. He supported his contention by noting that the bee (or hornet) was considered as a sacred symbol of the Pharaohs.[32] There are two principal objections to this view. First, the sending of the "hornet" was still future on the eve of the conquest (Deut. 7:20). Second, there is no evidence that the Egyptians had a serious interest in the region of Transjordan at this time. The Amorites may have been defeated in Transjordan, but they were still a major threat in the land of Canaan.

The other view is preferable, for it regards the expression as figurative, referring to the panic-producing power of God which overcame both Sihon and Og. This suggestion is supported by Exodus 23:27-30; Deuteronomy 2:25 and 7:20. The prophecy of the "hornet" in Exodus 23:27-28 seems to further support this view, for the two verses are in synonomous parallelism. The expressions "terror" and "hornet" appear to refer to the same idea. That this view is historically correct can be argued from Joshua 2:9, 11 and Joshua 5:1. Rahab clearly testified to the panic produced by the fear that the Canaanites had for Israel.

The stipulations of this covenant renewal are recorded in verses 14-24. They included the obligations imposed upon, and accepted by, the vassal. The heart of the matter is observed in verse 14. Two things are required of Israel: (1) to fear Jehovah, and (2) to serve Him. Joshua was careful to define what the nature of that service was to be. First of all, it should be sincere, and then it should be founded on truth. It is not enough for one merely to serve God in sincerity. If the service is not founded on, and conditioned by, the truth of Scripture, it is worthless activity. True service also involves separation, thus the children of Israel were commanded to put away the gods which were among them (cf. v. 15 ff.). The people agreed

---

[32]John Garstang, *Joshua-Judges: The Foundations of Bible History* (New York: Richard R. Smith, Inc., 1931), p. 259.

to these stipulations, and Joshua reminded them of the tremendous obligation that was theirs in the light of this commitment.

The final portion of the covenant renewal involved the writing down of the agreement and depositing that covenant in a place where it could be observed and read (vv. 25-28).

The death of Joshua is described in the remaining verses of this chapter. At the age of 110, he passed off the scene of Israelite history. He was buried in his inheritance in the mountains of Ephraim. During his lifetime, the children of Israel remained faithful to the Lord (v. 31). A fitting conclusion to the story of Joshua would be the words of Psalm 44:1-3, "We have heard with our ears, O God, our fathers have told us, what work thou didst in their days, in the times of old. How thou didst drive out the heathen with thy hand, and plantedst them; how thou didst afflict the people, and cast them out. For they got not the land in possession by their own sword, neither did their own arm save them: but thy right hand, and thine arm, and the light of thy countenance, because thou hadst a favor unto them."

JUDGES

Chapter 7

FAILURE AND ITS CAUSES
(Judges 1:1—3:4)

In the Book of Joshua the *survival* and the *success* of the nation of Israel during the years of conquest are the dominant themes. The Book of Judges, on the other hand, emphasizes the religious and military struggles of this nation during its long period of settlement in the land.

I. INTRODUCTION

A. *The Title of the Book*

The Hebrew title of the book is *šopᵉtîm* ("judges"). This title is based on the type of leadership Israel experienced between the days of the elders who ruled after Joshua and the rise of King Saul. The establishment of the office of judge was first mentioned by Moses (Deut. 16:18; 17:9; 19:17). A *šopēt* was to stand by the side of the high priest as the supreme judge or leader in Israel. The function of the office of judge included more than mere civil service activities. In many cases their responsibilities included leadership in both military and religious affairs. Generally they were summoned directly to their work by divine appointment (cf. 3:15; 4:6; 6:12; etc.). The majority of judges functioned more in the role of "deliverer" from foreign oppression than as a civil judge. After deliverance was accomplished, the judge became a civil leader.

B. *Authorship and Date*

According to the Babylonian Talmud, Samuel was the author of the book. But there is no specific or conclusive evidence to support this claim. On the basis of the nature of the content of this book and its chronological notices, it is possible to say that Samuel may have written portions of the book with final additions by one of his students. Liberal criticism considers this book to be Deuteronomic in its present form (i.e., about 550 B.C. it supposedly received its final revision).

The date of composition was probably sometime in the early days of the united monarchy. The frequent expression, "In those days there was no king in Israel" (17:6; 18:1; 19:1; 21:25), indicates that the book was written after the establishment of the monarchy under Saul. According to 1:21 the Jebusites still controlled Jerusalem. This would place the time of writing before David's capture of the city about 990 B.C. (cf. II Sam. 5:6 ff., I Chron. 11:4-9). When the book was written, the Canaanites were still in control of Gezer (1:29) which would place the writing sometime before Solomon's reign, for the Egyptians captured the city and Pharaoh gave it to Solomon as a wedding gift (I Kings 9:16). Furthermore, it should be observed at this point that some portions of the book present material which seems to antedate the time of David. For example, Sidon was regarded as the chief city of Phoenicia rather than Tyre. This points to a time before the twelfth century B.C. With all evidence in view, it appears that the Book of Judges was most likely written sometime in the latter days of Saul or in the early days of David.

C. *Major Themes*

The principal theme of the Book of Judges is "Failure through Compromise" which is in contrast to the main theme in the Book of Joshua which was "Victory through Faith." The Book of Judges is a commentary on the nature and characteristics of spiritual apostasy. The writer not only presents the theological trends involved in apostasy, but vividly describes the practical consequences of apostasy in every-day life. The covenant failures of Israel are contrasted with the covenant faithfulness of Jehovah. The key verse of the Book of Judges is 17:6 which says, "In those days there was no king in Israel, but every man did that which was right in his own eyes" (cf. 21:25). Moral and spiritual relativism led to anarchy in those days.

D. *Historical Setting*

The events described in the Book of Judges cover a period which begins about 1380 B.C. and lasts until the rise of Saul in 1043 B.C. (see chart, p. 16). During the reign of the elders, and in the early period of the Judges (Othniel's judgeship and the oppression under Eglon of Moab), Egypt remained weak under the leadership of Akhnaton, Tutankhamon and Ay (c. 1377-1345 B.C.). Horemheb was able to consolidate some of Egypt's forces, but real military revival took place during the Nineteenth Dynasty (c. 1318-1222 B.C.). During the Ramasside age there was renewed interest in Palestine. The Pharaohs of this period increased and improved Egyptian military garrisons in Palestine. The victory stele of Merneptah (c. 1234-1222 B.C.) records a successful campaign and among the defeated peoples he lists Israel. The stele reads, "Israel is laid waste, his seed is not."[33]

There are two other Egyptian documents that shed interesting light on this period. The first is a satirical letter describing the journey of an Egyptian envoy through Syria and Palestine. The document is generally dated in the second half of the thirteenth century B.C. It describes the roads of Palestine as being overgrown with cypresses, oaks and cedars that were very tall, thereby making travel rather difficult. It makes mention of the fact that lions were numerous, thus confirming some of the details of the Samson story (Judg. 14:5, cf. also I Sam. 17:34). The envoy twice encountered thieves, indicating the difficulty of unhindered travel (cf. Judg. 5:6-7). One night they stole his horse and clothing, and on another occasion, his bow, sheath knife, and quiver. The story reveals that the writer had considerable knowledge of Palestinian geography. Most significant among the details of the document, however, are the many reflections of the unsettled conditions in the land and the problem with robbers and thieves. This story reflects the same situation described in Judges. "Every man did that which was right in his own eyes."

The other document of interest to us is known as the story of Wenamon. Wenamon was a temple official sent to Byblos, a Phoenician port city, to purchase cedar for the bark of Amen. He received his orders from Heri-Hor, a priest-king residing in

---

[33]James B. Pritchard (ed.), *Ancient Near Eastern Texts*, "Hymn of Victory of Mer-ne-Ptah" Trans. John A. Wilson (New Jersey: Princeton University Press, 1955), p. 378. (Hereafter referred to as *ANET*).

Thebes. When he reached the Palestinian coast, he was robbed before reaching his destination. He received no cooperation from the local kings he encountered. In fact, he was humiliated on many occasions. All this probably indicates the growing independence of Syrian and Palestinian monarchs. Egypt at this time was suffering from internal struggles and did not have the prestige it formerly enjoyed in Palestine. The date generally assigned to this document is the first half of the eleventh century B.C. Again this sheds light on the general political conditions of the Judges period.[34]

One of the arch enemies of Egypt during this time was the Hittite empire (c. 1400-c. 1200 B.C.). After a series of struggles the two countries concluded a peace treaty.[35] Not many years after this treaty, the Hittite empire, like other lands, fell to the "Sea Peoples." The Egyptians, under the reign of Ramses III (1190 B.C.-1164 B.C.), repulsed an attempted invasion of the Delta area by these "Sea Peoples" among whom the Philistines were numbered. After their defeat in Egypt, many settled along the southwest coast of Palestine, thus joining the earlier Minoan settlers of the area (the "Philistines" of Abraham's day).

The power of Egypt as well as other surrounding nations was used by God to awaken Israel out of the deep sleep of apostasy which set in many times during the Judges period. The apostasies of Israel paved the way for her powerful enemies to oppress her. When Israel repented, leaders were raised up and the nation was delivered from the oppression.

E. *The Literary Structure of the Book*

The chapters of the Book of Judges are not arranged in strict chronological sequence. Chapters 1 and 2 contain the introduction to the period. Chapters 3 through 16 describe the period of judgeships and oppressions. The last four chapters are an appendix to the book and describe events which occurred before or during the judgeship of Othniel. The reason for plac-

---

[34]See *ANET*, "The Journey of Wen-Amon to Phoenicia" Trans. John A. Wilson, p. 25 ff.

[35]*ANET*, "Treaty Between Hattusilis and Ramses II" Trans. Albrecht Goetze, p. 201ff.

ing these events before Chapter 4 of the book will be discussed later.[36] The following chart will help in understanding the literary structure of the book.

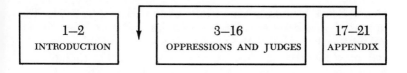

| 1—2 | 3—16 | 17—21 |
| INTRODUCTION | OPPRESSIONS AND JUDGES | APPENDIX |

F. Basic Outline

1. The Record of Incomplete Conquest (1:1—3:4)
2. The Oppressions and the Judges (3:5—16:31)
3. Appendix: The Period of Tribal Disorder (17:1—21:25)

II. THE RECORD OF INCOMPLETE CONQUEST (1:1-2:23)

A. The Political-Military Situation

1. Judah and the Kenites (1:1-20)

The Book of Judges begins the same way the Book of Joshua does; namely, with the death of a great leader. In Joshua 1:1 the death of Moses marked the end of the wilderness journey and the beginning of the conquest era. Judges 1:1 records the death of Joshua and therefore marks the period of tribal settlement in the land. The first phase of the conquest had been completed under Joshua; now the phase of settlement and colonization would begin. This marked the beginning of a very long, slow process covering a period of about 350 years. The question raised in verse one reflects the principal concern of the tribes at this time, ". . . who shall go up for us against the Canaanites?" The term "Canaanites" here is used in a broad, inclusive sense involving all the ethnic groups of Canaan. The selection of Judah (v. 2) is appropriate since it was the larger of the tribes and occupied one of the largest territories. Simeon joined with Judah in the settlement of the South as would be

---

[36]*Infra.* p. 147

expected since Simeon's allotment was with that of Judah (Josh. 19:1).

The initial efforts of Judah and Simeon were successful as indicated by verses 4-7. One important battle was fought at the site of Bezek located in the vicinity of Jerusalem (cf. v. 7). The armies of Bezek were badly defeated, losing 10,000 men (v. 4). Adoni-Bezek, leader of the Canaanite forces, was able to escape but only for a short time. Upon his capture his thumbs and great toes were cut off (v. 6), a practice designed to render one useless for military service. The principle of *Lex Taliones* was employed in this case and Adoni-Bezek recognized this (v. 7). Following this, Judah captured Jerusalem (v. 8) but did not maintain control of the city (cf. v. 21). The city was regarded as a foreign city in 19:11, 12. It was not until the time of David that the city came under permanent Israelite control. The military victories· of the Kenites are enumerated in verses 11-16. Many of the events described in this chapter must have taken place before the death of Joshua (cf. Josh. 15:13-20). The Kenites were dwelling in the Jericho area according to verse 16. The expression "city of palm trees" is either a reference to Jericho itself or areas immediately adjacent to it (cf. 3:13 with Deut. 34:3 and II Chron. 28:15). It will be remembered that the curse Joshua placed upon Jericho applied to refortification of the city, not mere habitation.

Judah was successful in achieving most of its initial goals which included the hill country around Hebron (v. 9; Heb. *hāhār*), the steppe areas to the desert in the south (Heb. *hanegeḇ*; v. 9) and the foothills leading toward the coast to the west (v. 9; Heb. *hašepēlāh*. Due to the effective deployment of iron reinforced chariots by the Canaanites (v. 19; cf. 4:3; Josh. 17:16; I Sam. 13:19), they were unable to conquer the larger valleys.

2. *Benjamin* (1:21)

While Benjamin probably occupied most of its alloted territory, it was unable to gain control of Jerusalem which was under strong Jebusite control (v. 21). The expression "unto this day" reveals that the account was penned before David's capture of the city.

3. *Manasseh and Ephraim* (1:22-29)

The failures of Ephraim and Manasseh were largely due to their disobedience in not destroying Canaanite settlements in their territory. Rather than total destruction as God had commanded, they enslaved the Canaanites and put them to "tribute," better translated "taskwork or labor gangs" (Heb. *mas;* note v. 28). Gezer, according to verse 29, remained in the hands of the Canaanites. This was evidently the case until a Pharaoh of Solomon's day captured it and gave it to him as a wedding gift (I Kings 9:16).

4. *The Remaining Tribes* (1:30-36)

Many of the other tribes adopted the same policies as the tribe of Manasseh in that they did not destroy their enemy, but used him to increase their wealth (cf. vv. 30, 33). The tribe of Asher merely moved in among the Canaanites without attempting to control their area (cf. v. 32). Because of the strength of the Amorites in the valleys to the west, the Danites were restricted to the mountains (v. 34). This led to eventual frustration and the search for new territory in the north (18:1-31).

B. *The Religious Situation* (2:1-23)

1. *The Reasons for Failure* (2:1-15)

a. *Religious Life in the Days of Joshua* (2:1-9)

Chapter 2 presents an interesting comparison in Israelite religious life during the days of Joshua and after the death of Joshua when a new generation had control of the nation. In the days of Joshua, divine rebuke met with a spirit of repentance (2:1-6), resulting in service to Jehovah (v. 7). The people of Joshua's day had witnessed the miraculous workings of their God and had constant reminders of their covenant responsibilities (Josh. 8:30-35; 18:1-7; 23:1—24:28).

When the angel of the Lord spoke to the people at Bochim (v. 1, a site probably located in the vicinity of Shiloh), there was a clear emphasis upon Jehovah's covenant faithfulness and

3644

the obvious disobedience of the nation (v. 2). Israel remained faithful to Jehovah during the days of Joshua and the period when the elders ruled after Joshua (v. 7). This does not mean that there were no times of failure and apostasy for this is quite clearly the case as intimated in Joshua's farewell address to the nation (Josh. 24:24 ff.).

b. *Religious Life after the Days of Joshua and the Elders* (2:10-15)

After the death of Joshua and the elders which followed him, a new generation arose which had been exposed to Canaanite culture from birth. This generation had not witnessed the great miracles performed by God for His people in the initial conquest (v. 10). Their parents did not evidently exercise a very strong godly influence on this generation, for it had turned aside to the worship of "Baalim" (v. 11). The term "Baalim" was probably used to describe all the false deities of the land and would therefore be synonymous with the expression "other gods." The principal gods of Canaan which this new generation worshipped are named in verse 13. Baal was one of the most popular gods in the Canaanite pantheon. This is attested by both Ugaritic and Biblical literature. Baal was the fertility god who rode upon the clouds and was responsible for the rains which brought life to the parched soil of Canaan. In Ugaritic mythology he was called the "son of Dagon" (cf. I Sam. 5:1-7; Judg. 16:23).[37]

Ashtoreth appears as Athtart in Ugaritic literature. In the Old Testament the name appears in both singular and plural forms (sing. Ashtoreth, pl. Ashtaroth, cf. I Kings 11:5; also I Sam. 31:10). She entered the Greek world by way of Cyprus and later became known as Astarte (Aphrodite of classical mythology). She was the Canaanite goddess of generation and fertility. She was also considered as a goddess of war. Ishtar was her Assyro-Babylonian counterpart.

The Canaanite cultic practices relating to the worship of Baal and Ashtoreth are well known to us through recent discoveries. Their system included animal sacrifices, in many cases

---

[37] *ANET,* "Poems about Baal and Anath" Trans. H. G. Ginsberg, pp. 130, 142.

Baal-Hadad (Jupiter-Helios) from ruins of Baalbek in Lebanon. Levant Photo Service

using the same animals as Israel did in her sacrifices.[38] Temple prostitution was a widespread practice and one that was thoroughly degrading. Moses was careful to warn against such a practice (Deut. 23:17). Fertility rites using libations of wine, oil, and so on, were common in attempting to assure fertility of the land. In some places human sacrifice was practiced. The more one studies the activities involved in the worship of Baal, the clearer it becomes as to why Jehovah demanded complete destruction of this religious system and its followers.

The question that needs to be raised at this point is, "Why did Israel fall prey to this sensuous form of worship when she had such a lofty revelation of the true God and clear standards of moral conduct?" Several answers may be given to this question. First, the gradual fragmentation of the tribes contributed to an abandonment of Shiloh as the only center of worship. As previously noted, the principal unifying factor in Israel was her religion and commitment to one place of worship. As the tribes moved into new territories rather than defeating their enemy, they sought ways to establish peaceful coexistence with them. This was probably the case as tribes moved down into the valleys where Canaanite religious and cultural influence was the greatest. Secondly, Baalism may have had a pragmatic appeal. The Israelites who attempted to farm in the hill country must have experienced some frustration and looked with envy on the beautiful crops of their Canaanite neighbors in the fertile valleys. The temptation to look to Baal to increase in fertility was always there and many fell to it. In this connection notice the words of Jeremiah (44:17-19). Thirdly, the sensuous appeal of temple prostitution would have allured some into Canaanite practices. Finally, the quest for political compatability led many to recognize the gods of Canaan through formal treaties. Intermarriage also led to formal recognition of the gods and gradual infiltration of pagan ideas into the community of Israel. Religious syncretism was slow, subtle, and disastrous.

2. The Remedy for Failure (2:16)

In order to provide spiritual and military leadership for Is-

---

[38]ANET, Ibid., "Keret" A: II:60 ff., p. 143.

rael, the Lord raised up judges. This provision, however, was in many cases rejected or ignored by apostate Israel (v. 17).

3. *The Response of Israel* (2:17-19)

The recognition and worship of other gods continued in spite of divine warning and admonition. Verse 17 describes the activity of unbelieving Israel as "whoring after other gods." In the light of the nature of Canaanite temple worship, this expression is most appropriate. In effect, the tender mercy of God and His gracious provisions were trampled down in high-handed rebellion. This was indeed a dark hour in the history of Israel. From the *triumphal conquest* of Joshua we are now brought face to face with the *tragic crisis* in the days of the Judges.

4. *The Rebuke from Jehovah* (2:20—3:4)

Because Israel had broken her covenant with Jehovah (v. 20), the Lord promised that He would no longer drive out the nations before her as He had done before (v. 21). The nations would remain there to test Israel (v. 22; 3:1, 4). This new generation would learn of war because of this (3:2). Among the main enemies of Israel were the five "lords" of the Philistines (v. 3). The Hebrew word for "lord" (*seren*) is always used in connection with the Philistines with one exception. Most scholars feel that this is a Philistine loan word.

C. *Practical Considerations*

Someone once said, "If I could just see a miracle performed by God I know my faith would be established and never waver." This sounds like a reasonable statement at first, but after careful examination, it will be seen to be faulty. If visible miracles were really the solution to weak faith, then Israel should have been an unshakable nation spiritually. No other people on the face of the earth have ever witnessed more miracles and yet they were led astray. Remember that during the days of Christ here on earth, men witnessed many miracles but they still refused to believe. We are reminded of the words of Hebrews 11:1, "Faith is the substance of things hoped for, the evidence of things not seen. . . ."

A second lesson to be learned from these opening chapters is that spiritual and theological apostasy is a subtle process. Merely being in possession of a correct theology does not guarantee freedom from crisis. There must be a consistent application of divine truth in the life of the believer in order to be assured of a job well done and a battle well fought (II Tim. 4:7).

Chapter 8

GAINS AND LOSSES
(Judges 3:5–9:59)

Whatever glory the people of Israel experienced in the days of Joshua, and the days of the elders which followed, quickly disappeared under the crushing defeats brought about by Israel's apostasy. Judges 3—19 are an enlightening commentary on the fortunes of Israel during the fourteenth and thirteenth centuries B.C. This period was characterized by recurring cycles of spiritual apostasy, oppression from foreign nations, repentance on the part of the people, and deliverance achieved through the leadership of divinely appointed judges. A bird's-eye view of the situation can be gained by study of the following chart.

Chart of the Oppressions

Nation	Time	Delivering Judge
Mesopotamia, under Cushan-rishathaim	Eight years	Othniel
Moab, under King Eglon	Eighteen years	Ehud
Philistines	?	Shamgar
Canaanites, under Jabin of Hazor	Twenty years	Deborah and Barak
Midian	Seven years	Gideon
?	?	Tola
?	?	Jair
Ammonites	Eighteen years	Jephthah
?	?	Ibzan
?	?	Elon
?	?	Abdon
Philistines	Forty years	Samson

I. OTHNIEL – THE FIRST JUDGE (3:5-11)

A. *Oppression from the Northeast* (vv. 5-8)

One of the factors leading to national apostasy was the widespread intermarriage between the Israelites and the Canaanites

in the land. One of the results of such intermarriage was a recognition of the gods of the Canaanites (v. 6). This apostasy
led them to abandon their worship of Jehovah and serve Baalim
and the "groves." The true meaning of the original Hebrew
word is not fully conveyed by the translation "groves," for
the Bible describes "groves" as being carried out of the
house of the Lord (see II Kings 23:6). The Hebrew expression
'ašērāh apparently refers to some kind of a wooden pole or perhaps a tree trunk which would have been set up beside a heathen
altar and used as an object of worship. It is probable that such
an object was regarded as the dwelling place of a deity (cf.
Deut. 16:21 and II Kings 17:10). Evidently the father of Gideon
had such an object in his sanctuary (Judg. 6:26). Others were
located in Samaria, Jerusalem, and Bethel (II Kings 13:6; 23:
6, 15). The tablets discovered at Ugarit (Ras Shamra) reveal
the fact that one of the popular Canaanite goddesses was given
this same name. This goddess was represented as a mother of
the gods and frequently had the title "Lady of the Sea."

In order to bring this idolatry to an end, the Lord permitted
a king by the name of Chushan-rishathaim from Mesopotamia to
oppress Israel for eight years (v. 8). The king's name literally
means "doubly wicked Chushan." It is felt by many that this
is an epithet assigned to him by his enemies. It is also possible,
however, that the word "rishathaim" is a Hebraized form of a
foreign word, perhaps a place-name.[39]

B. *A Deliverer Appointed* (vv. 9-11)

After eight years of servitude under Cushan-rishathaim, the
children of Israel again looked to their God (v. 9). The Lord
heard their cry and raised up a deliverer by the name Othniel,
the son-in-law of Caleb. Othniel was a good choice because
he had wide experience in warfare, having shared in the conquest of Canaan. He was previously known for his heroism at
Kirjath-sepher (Josh. 15:15-20 and Judg. 1:13 ff.). He was
from the tribe of Judah and therefore would have gained rather
wide support for his campaigns.

---

[39]Charles F. Pfeiffer, "Judges" *The Wycliffe Bible Commentary* (Chicago: Moody Press, 1962), p. 239.

The preparations for the office of judge and the functions of that office are clearly delineated in verse 10. In spite of the wide military experience of Othniel, he still needed additional divine help for the tremendous task at hand. In order to prepare him adequately, the Spirit of God empowered him in a special way for the task. This ministry of the Spirit should not be confused with regeneration which is permanent in nature and brings a change in life and character. The empowerment in these cases was for a special task and did not necessarily produce any moral transformation in the individual (cf. I Sam. 16:14 with Ps. 51:11). The responsibilities of the office of judge were basically twofold: (1) a civil responsibility involving the "judging" of Israel, and (2) a military responsibility; that is, to lead Israel against the enemy which had oppressed them (v. 10). The efforts of Othniel were successful and Israel was freed from the oppressing hand of Chushan-rishathaim. Following this deliverance Israel enjoyed forty years of rest (v. 11).

II. EHUD — A GIFTED BENJAMITE (vv. 12-30)

After forty years of freedom from foreign domination, however, Israel again forgot the penalty for idolatry. According to verse 12, they repeated the apostasy for which they had been punished earlier, and the Lord, therefore, raised up another oppressor in the person of Eglon, king of Moab. Approximately 1335 B.C., the Moabites conducted a successful campaign in the area of Transjordan. Presumably they defeated portions of the eastern tribes and then were able to move down into the Jordan Valley and establish a provincial capital at Jericho described in verse 13 as the "city of palm trees." The Moabites were not alone in this conquest. According to verse 13, Eglon allied himself with the Ammonites (whose kingdom lay to the north of Moab) and with the Amalekites, who were migrant nomads to the south. For eighteen years Eglon, king of Moab, enjoyed military supremacy on the east bank of the Jordan and in the Jordan Valley. After eighteen years, Israel began to realize the helplessness of their situation. Again they were forced to cry unto their God for deliverance. Even though they had betrayed His trust once, God, in His mercy, listened to their cry and raised up a deliverer, this time, however, from the tribe of Benjamin rather than from the large tribe of Judah. The tribe of Benjamin had probably suffered the greatest at the hands of the Moabites. It was, therefore, appropriate that the leader should come from that tribe.

Another detail is given to us about Ehud in verse 15; namely, that he was left-handed. This seems to be a characteristic of the Benjamites as noted in Judges 20:16. In I Chronicles 12:2 they are described as being ambidextrous. Being left-handed would be an advantage for Ehud in the situation in which he found himself, for a left-handed person would bind his dagger on the opposite side to that on which it was usually carried, a distinct aid in concealing the weapon. The pretext which he used to gain access to Eglon, king of Moab, was the delivering of the yearly tribute described in verse 15 as a "present." In preparation for the trip, Ehud made a dagger which had two edges and measured a cubit in length (v. 16). The Hebrew word for "cubit" here is unique and not used elsewhere in the Old Testament. It is the word *gomed*. Some judge this dagger to have been about one foot long. King Eglon is described in this chapter as a "very fat man" (v. 17). It is not usual for the Bible to indulge in personal descriptions; however, such a description is necessary to the understanding of the events that follow; namely, verse 22. Ehud went down through Gilgal to Jericho, and there came in contact with Eglon, who was at that time sitting in "a summer parlor" (v. 20). This summer parlor was probably an upper room of the building which would provide some fresh air. Ehud announced that he had "a message from God." The importance of this statement was immediately realized by Eglon, and the Bible says that he arose out of his seat, which for him may have been quite a chore. Following this, Ehud removed the dagger and thrust it into the corpulent king — a most unusual employment of visual aids announcing the "message from God" (v. 20)! Considerable time elapsed before the servants discovered the assassination, and certainly much too late, for Ehud had escaped, returned to his territory, and had given a call to arms (v. 27). The children of Israel took advantage of this situation, and as a result, under the leadership

of Ehud, brought eighty years of freedom from foreign oppression (v. 30).

III. SHAMGAR — OUTSTANDING WARRIOR (3:31)

Shamgar is described as "the son of Anath." This is somewhat
problematic, since Anath was the name of the Canaanite goddess of sex and war, and the sister of Baal. However, in the light
of the idiomatic use of the expression "son of" the expression
may be interpreted to mean "the warrior." Shamgar lived in
the latter days of Ehud and the early days of Deborah and
Barak (cf. 5:6). He lived in a time when the highways were
unoccupied, and the travelers had to walk through narrow side
paths because of the dangers throughout the land. His exploits
were directed principally against the Philistines of whom he
slew 600 with an ox goad. This number may represent a life-
long total rather than a single battle. The ox goad which was
employed in such fighting was an instrument used for urging
oxen forward, and measured as much as eight feet long.
They were normally pointed at one end with a metal tip and
had a chisel shaped blade on the other end for scraping a plow
share. Such goads could be used effectively in the place of a
spear. It was a humble weapon indeed, but then God many
times uses humble things to accomplish His purpose.

IV. DEBORAH AND BARAK — PARTNERS IN VICTORY
(Chapters 4 and 5)

A. *The Military Strength of Jabin* (4:1-3)

After eighty years of peace, Israel again grew careless in her
spiritual commitments and forsook the Lord their God. As a result, the Lord allowed Jabin, described as the king of Canaan
reigning in Hazor, to overrun the northern territories of Israel
and to bring the nation again under foreign domination. The
name "Jabin" was probably not a personal name, but a dynastic title (cf. Josh. 11:1 and Ps. 83:9). According to the records
in Joshua 11 the Israelites conquered the city of Hazor and killed
Jabin, king of that city. However, it seems that the Israelites,
even though gaining victory in the area, were not able to con-

solidate their position, and the Canaanites had quickly retaken and rebuilt the city. During the time of Joshua, Hazor was the head of the kingdoms in that area (Josh. 11:10). It is not impossible that Hazor achieved a similar position in the time of the Judges under the leadership of Jabin and his general, Sisera. Sisera is described as having dwelt in Harosheth of the Gentiles (4:2). This site is generally identified with modern Tell Amar located at the place where the Kishon River passes through a narrow gorge to enter the Plain of Acre. It is about ten miles northwest of the important city of Meggido. The military strength of the Canaanites was very impressive. In addition to thousands of foot soldiers, Sisera had under his control about 900 iron-reinforced chariots (cf. vv. 3, 13). This number of chariots is not out of proportion for that part of the country. Thutmoses III boasted of having captured 924 chariots among the spoils of the battle of Megiddo.[40]

B. *Preparations for Battle* (4:4-13)

Following the twenty years of oppression, the Lord raised up a prophetess and judge by the name of Deborah. Verse 5 indicates that she sat in judgment at a site somewhere between Ramah and Bethel in Mount Ephraim. The time came when battle preparations should be made and an attack should be prepared against Jabin and Sisera. She called on Barak, an experienced general from the tribe of Naphtali (v. 6). Using 10,000 men from the tribes of Naphtali and Zebulun (v. 6) and other tribes (5:14-15), he was to go to the area of the river Kishon and there meet Sisera and the Canaanite armies (v. 7). Barak refused to go without a prophetic complement; namely, the presence of Deborah. Barak should not be judged as lacking faith at this point. He merely wanted the one who could give divine guidance and help for such an important occasion. He was quickly reminded by Deborah that the victory which God would give would not come as a result of his genius, but in effect would be a victory brought by the Lord.

---

[40]*ANET*, "The Asiatic Campaigns of Thut-mose III" Trans. John A. Wilson, p. 237.

The ultimate downfall of Sisera, according to verse 9, would be at the hand of a woman — not Deborah, but Jael (vv. 18-21).

C. Encounter and Victory (4:14—5:31)

1. The Nature of the Battle (4:14-16)

The battle followed and the Scripture tells us that the Lord discomfited Sisera and his chariots (v. 15). At this point we are not given any details as to what method God used in immobilizing the chariot force of Sisera. However, in the victory hymn of Deborah and Barak, recorded in Chapter 5 of this book, an additional clue is given. In verse 21 we are informed that the river Kishon "swept them away." We might suppose from this that the Lord brought rains, thereby flooding parts of the valley floor and causing the chariots to be immobilized. Recent history has given us additional light on the nature of such an event. Torrents of water contributed to the defeat of the Turks in this very area in April of 1799 when numbers of their fleeing troops were swept away and drowned. During World War I, English troops found that fifteen minutes of rain on the clay soil rendered cavalry maneuvers almost impossible.

2. The Flight of Sisera (4:17-24)

As the battle continued, Sisera recognized the hopelessness of his situation. When his chariot was no longer able to move, he fled away on foot (v. 17). On his way northward, he came to the tent dwelling of Jael, the wife of Heber the Kenite. He fully expected protection from this small clan of Kenites, for they had joined peaceably with the Canaanites in that area. Remember that the Kenites originally were settled in the area of Hebron along with Caleb (Josh. 14:10-15; 15:15-20; Judg. 1:16). Evidently Jael was not in agreement with the coalition made by her husband and others with the Canaanites and used this occasion to express her dissatisfaction. She invited Sisera to her tent for refreshment and rest, as would be the normal custom in the Ancient Near East. However, once asleep, she took a tent peg and a mallet and brought his life to an end (v. 21). The great victory accomplished on that day was not due to the genius of Barak, nor to the aggressiveness of Jael, but — according to verse 23 — the power of God. This victory brought peace and prosperity to Israel for about forty years (4:24; 5:31).

3. *The Song of Praise* (5:1-31)

The song of victory recorded in this chapter was, in all probability, written by Deborah. It is a song expressing praise to God for His intervention in behalf of His people. It recognizes His great patience in the light of Israel's infidelity. Even though written in highly poetic style utilizing very difficult archaic Hebrew words, it none the less is a song of beauty and one that provides us with very interesting details about Israel's past history. For example, in verse 4 it describes the Lord bringing rains during the days of the wilderness wandering. This information sheds important light on Israel's survival during this period. Living conditions in the days of Shamgar and Jael are also described in verse 6. The highways were unoccupied because the enemy controlled them. This was a time of open idolatry, for Israel "chose new gods" (v. 8). This was also a time of tribal independence, for not all the tribes participated in the war against Sisera. Verses 15-17 list Reuben, Gilead, Dan, and Asher as those who refused to join in this battle. The reference to Dan as remaining in ships (v. 17) is interesting and enlightening. It implies that the migration of the Danites recorded in Judges 18 had taken place prior to the time of Deborah and that the Danites had experienced some degree of amalgamation with the seafaring Phoenicians to the northwest. After a brief description of the battle in poetic form (vv. 19-27), the writer then gives us a look into the household of Sisera. The feminine touch is obviously present here as the emotions and the reactions of the mother of Sisera are viewed. It is the feeling of many that this indeed represents the hand of Deborah.

V. GIDEON — MAN OF VALOR (6:1—9:56)

A. *The Midianite Oppression* (6:1-10)

The Nature of the Oppression (6:2-7)

As a result of Israelite apostasy (v. 1) and open disobedience to God's commands (v. 10), they were delivered into the hands of the Midianites and the "sons of the east" (v. 3) who came from the eastern desert regions. These nomadic peoples ranged from the southern part of the Sinai peninsula (Exod. 3:1) northward to the gulf of Aqabah (I Kings 11:18) and as far as the plains east of Moab (Gen. 36:35; Num. 22:4; 25:1, 6; Josh. 13:21). The Midianites were related to the Hebrews in so much as Midian was a son of Abraham by his second wife, Keturah (Gen. 25:1-6). Joining the Midianites in their raids from the east were the Amalekites and the "children of the east" (v. 3). Since the "children of the east" were probably no-mads from a Syrian desert, it was appropriate that these people should employ camels for their military needs rather than horses and chariots (cf. v. 5). It appears that the Midianite invaders destroyed many of the crops of Israel, and for seven years Israel did not realize full productivity (cf. vv. 6-7). The result of seven years of frustration and even starvation was that Israel again cried to their God (v. 7). In response, the Lord sent a prophet who issued a severe warning and rebuke to the people of Israel (vv. 8-10). While there is the expression of Jehovah's extreme hatred for sin in the earlier verses of this chapter, we are also reminded of Jehovah's great love for the sinner in the fact that He provided a prophet and a judge to bring deliverance.

B. *The Call of Gideon* (6:11-40)

The character and the actions of Gideon are not always sub-ject to easy analysis as is evident from the various views re-garding this man. Some consider him a weak, insecure man and therefore lacking real faith. Others consider him a great cham-pion of faith. Only a careful analysis of the verses that follow will help to solve this problem. Gideon, like most Israelites at that time, lived in fear as evidenced by the fact that he threshed his wheat beside the winepress in order to avoid detection by the Midianites. It was there that he encountered the angel of the Lord (Heb. *mal'ak yahweh*). This expression is best un-derstood as describing a theophany. It represents the same type of encounter recorded in 2:1-5. The first thing pointed out to Gideon was that the Lord was with him (v. 12). This statement, however, presented a theological problem to Gideon, for he asked, "If the Lord be with us, why then is all this befallen us?" (v. 13). In other words, "If God is on our side, why have we experienced seven years of tragedy?" Of course, the answer to this should have been obvious to Gideon. It was the wickedness of his people that brought destruction and despair. The Lord then challenged Gideon to be Israel's new leader. Like Moses (Exod. 4:1, 10), Gideon found excuses as to why he did not qualify for the responsibility. Gideon was probably nearing middle age at this time since he had a son in his teens (8:20). He also pointed out that his family was "poor in Manasseh" (v. 15), which probably referred to the military weakness which characterized the tribe of Manasseh. In addition to that, he was the least — that is, the youngest — in his father's house. Gideon was then given a sign as a confirmation of God's claim upon his life (cf. Exod. 4:2-9).

While we might agree that Gideon was weak in faith at this point, we should not consider him a man of no faith whatsoever. The sign which God provided for him required that he bring certain things before the angel of the Lord. These objects included valuable food stuffs (cf. v. 19), and during a time of famine, it would indeed take an act of faith on the part of Gideon to use such material. This faith on the part of Gideon was honored by God in that fire consumed the offering brought on that occasion (v. 21). Gideon immediately recognized that the visitor to whom he had been speaking was the Lord himself (v. 22), and he had great fear because to see God would probably mean certain death (Exod. 33:20). The real test of Gideon was yet to follow. The fact that he did make a definite commitment to his God is evidenced in his going to his father's own house and destroying the altars of Baal along with the grove that was built beside it (v. 25). This portion of Scripture is also a sad commentary on the tribe of Manasseh, for here was located a private sanctuary dedicated to Baal and Asherah. Perhaps most disheartening is the reaction of the men who lived in that town, for when they discovered that the sanctuary dedicated to Baal had been destroyed, they sought the life of Gideon. It is ironic indeed that the Israelites were willing to take the life of a man who destroyed a pagan altar (v. 30). Even though

Gideon's father was probably a worshipper of Baal previously, it appears that he joined Gideon in his stand for the true faith (v. 31). His arguments in behalf of Gideon are effective. He charged that if Baal were really a god, let him defend himself. Why should a man have to save his god? It ought to be the other way around; namely, the god saving individual man. With this responsibility cared for, Gideon now had to face the principal task at hand; that is, the threat of the Midianites and Amalekites.

Gideon, like Othniel (3:10), was prepared by the Holy Spirit in a special way for the task at hand (v. 34). The original text at this point, however, is different from that which describes the experience of Othniel. Here the Hebrew word for "come upon" is *lābe̊šāh*. This verb literally means "to clothe"; in other words, the Spirit of God clothed Gideon. With this strength he began to marshal the armies of Israel. But, again, Gideon wanted divine assurance that he was within the will of God and had clearly understood God's directives. Therefore, he required another sign. He suggested that a fleece be placed on the stone threshing floor, and if the dew remained only on the fleece and the earth was dry around it, he would consider this as a sign from God. When this was fulfilled, he considered the matter again and realized that it was not unnatural for the dew to remain on the fleece, whereas the ground would quickly dry up in the sun (vv. 36-37). Therefore, he requested a second sign or confirmation of God's will. This time the process was reversed, and the fleece was dry and the ground around it remained wet with the dew after the sunrise (v. 39). With these signs Gideon was assured of God's directives in the matter of warfare.

C. *Selecting the Troops* (7:1-15)

Along the foothills of Mount Gilboa, Gideon began to marshal the troops together. When his army was organized, he had 32,000 men which was a small number compared to the Midianite coalition which numbered 135,000 (8:10). Gideon's faith was again tested, for the Lord told him that he had too many soldiers. He was commanded to urge those who were

afraid to return home from the camp at Gilead. When the
message was given to the people, 22,000 returned home, leaving him with an army of only 10,000 men (v. 4). Again the
Lord spoke to him, and indicated that the army was still too
large and that it had to be reduced even further. This reduc-
tion took place at the place where the men would drink their
water. Those who bowed on their knees to drink were dis-
missed; whereas, those who lapped with their tongues "as a
dog lappeth" (v. 5) were kept in the army of Gideon. Those
who were kept appeared to be the ones who stood upright
while drinking the water from their hands, thus prepared for a
sudden attack. Josephus, however, interpreted the passage in
a different way. Rather than selecting the men who were most
fit from a military point of view for the battle, he argues that
the Lord chose the least fit from a military point of view in order
that the miracle might be greater.[41] After the army was organized, a third sign was given to Gideon to confirm the forth-
coming victory (vv. 13-14). Gideon expressed his thankful-
ness for the sign in the form of worship (v. 15).

D. The Victory over Midian (7:16–8:21)

The army was divided into three companies of 100 each (cf.
I Sam. 11:11). They were to carry torches covered by a clay
pot or jugglet of some kind. In the beginning of the middle
watch (v. 19), that is, a little before midnight, they were to
blow the trumpets and the pitchers were to be broken, thus
exposing the torches and producing great light. This surprise
maneuver was very effective, for the camels were probably fright-
ened and the men were turned one against the other (vv. 21-
22). The Lord used this to give Gideon the initial victory over
these armies in spite of the overwhelming odds. Once the
Midianite coalition was on the run, Gideon called additional help
from the other tribes to complete the battle. The narrative
actually ends with 7:24 and is not resumed until 8:4. There the
battles in the Jordan Valley and the area to the east are described. The intervening verses record the dissatisfaction of the
tribe of Ephraim in not being called during the initial stages of
the battle (8:1-3). Gideon responded to this dissatisfaction by

---

[41]*Ant.* V: 6:3.

commending them on their valor. Jephthah was not so kind, however, when the arrogant tribe of Ephraim later expressed similar dissatisfaction (cf. 12:1-15). Perhaps the tribe of Ephraim was not accustomed to taking second place in battle plans, especially since Joshua was an Ephraimite and was a great leader in Israel. The remaining portion of Chapter 8 describes the successful pursuit of the Midianite alliance toward the east and their ultimate defeat. Gideon did not receive cooperation from the eastern tribes however. They were afraid that the victory of Gideon was merely temporary and if they joined him, they would later be severely defeated by a reorganized army from the east (vv. 13-21). The result of Gideon's great victory was that the people of Israel wanted him to become king (v. 22). This he refused, for he considered God to be their King.

E. *The Last Days of Gideon* (8:22-35)

Unfortunately, the latter days of Gideon were marked by failure and apostasy. Gideon, along with the other Israelites who engaged in the battle, had access to tremendous quantities of riches taken from the Midianites (vv. 25-26). As a result of this, Gideon was led into cultic idolatry as evidenced by his making an ephod an object of worship (v. 27). He evidently was also involved in polygamous practices (cf. vv. 30-31). The last days of Gideon and the time shortly after his death were times of national decay according to verse 33. The decay and apostasy that characterized Israel's history at this time was also characteristic of the family of Gideon. This is reflected in the rebellion of one of his sons, recorded in Chapter 9.

F. *The Rebellion of Abimelech* (9:1-57)

Gideon's polygamous practices brought great sorrow to his family after his death. Gideon's son by a concubine (8:31) decided that kingship was a legitimate thing and that he was the best candidate. Evidently Abimelech's mother was from Shechem, for he returned to that site in order to gain popular support for his proposed reign over Israel (9:2-3). Such support he did receive both from the inhabitants and from the priest of the local shrine at Shechem (v. 4). The designs of Abimelech for the city of Shechem and the tribes in that area brought about the death of his brothers, with one exception (v. 5). In spite of the warning given to Shechem by Jotham, the youngest son of Gideon, the city made Abimelech king and for three years he reigned over that city (v. 22). It is doubtful that the reign of Abimelech gained recognition anywhere else than in the Shechem area, and even this was short lived. A spirit of arrogance and suspicion overtook both Abimelech and the men of Shechem. The life of Abimelech came to an end very much like the great general Sisera; that is, at the hand of a woman. According to verse 53, a certain woman cast the upper part of a millstone upon Abimelech's head. This did not bring immediate death and in order to save face, Abimelech called for his armor bearer to draw the sword and to slay him (cf. the death of Saul, I Sam. 31:3).

G. *Practical Considerations*

The story of Gideon is a study in contrast. It is an excellent example of what God can do with a man when he acts in faith. Military might, prestige, and wealth are not able to frustrate God's purposes for men. In spite of the impressive numbers and the military strength of the Midianites, Gideon was given victory. A second lesson worth noting in this story is the danger of failure in spite of initial victories. Gideon had enjoyed unparalleled success in military matters; however, the victory brought to him access to tremendous wealth, and this in turn led him astray spiritually. He turned to cultic practices, and the taking of many wives resulting in a major rebellion in Israel under Abimelech, one of his sons. The implications of this story should be obvious to the believer. Even though he might enjoy significant success in spiritual things, he should be aware of the fact that he is human and open to the subtle temptations of Satan. If a great man such as Gideon could be tempted and could fall, how much more should we take care that we stand in full obedience to the Word of God.

Chapter 9

JEPHTHAH'S VOW
(Judges 10—12)

After the turbulent reign of Abimelech over the city of She-chem, there was a period of relative peace under the leadership of two judges about whom we are told very little. The forty-five years following Abimelech's rebellion were probably peace-ful ones for the most part. There is evidence however, in 10:1, that some deliverance was necessary from outside oppression.

I. PROSPERITY AND PEACE (10:1-5)

A. *The Judgeship of Tola* (10:1-2)

Following the reign of Abimelech, Tola the son of Puah as-sumed leadership in Israel. Tola and his father were of the tribe of Issachar and were named after two of the sons of Issa-char (cf. Gen. 46:13; Num. 26:23). During the days of David, the Tola clan was known for its men of valor (I Chron. 7:1-2). So far as we know, Issachar was the only tribe to furnish a judge during this period. While we know little of the ministry of Tola, it is clear from verse 1 that he was raised up by God "to save" Israel (Heb. *lehošîaʿ*). His judgeship lasted for a period of twenty-three years after which he died and was buried in Shamir (v. 2).

B. *The Judgeship of Jair* (10:3-5)

The judgeship of Jair began about 1131 B.C. and lasted for twenty-two years (v. 3). This judge is described as a Gileadite (v. 35). Since his name was the same as that of one of Manasseh's sons (Num. 32:41), it is fair to assume that he came from that tribe. He was a man of considerable wealth and prosperity. He, like other of the judges, engaged in polygamy, for he is described as having thirty sons (v. 4). The evidence of his rank and prominence in the land is further indicated by the fact that his sons rode thirty ass colts (v. 4). The ass was highly esteemed as a riding beast and many times carried with it special recognition (Judg. 1:14; I Sam. 25:20). The judgeship of Jair was probably limited to the area of Gilead primarily. After his death, he was buried in Camon (v. 5).

II. APOSTASY AND OPPRESSION (10:6-18)

A. *The Nature of Israel's Sin* (v. 6)

While Jair was probably a successful and prosperous judge, there is no evidence that he exerted any strong spiritual influence among the eastern tribes. The same can be said for Tola who probably exercised his greatest power in the central hill country on the west banks of the Jordan River. With an obvious absence of strong, vital, spiritual leadership, Israel again began to turn to the gods of Canaan which included the Baalim and Ashtaroth (v. 6). The apostasy of this time included much more than the mere recognition of Canaanite deities. According to verse 6, the gods of Syria (Aram) were worshipped. These would have included Hadad, Baal, Mot, and Anath. The gods of Zidon would be basically those of Syria. In Moab, Chemosh was a prominent deity (I Kings 11:33) while in Ammon, Molech seems to have been popular (I Kings 11:7, 33). The Philistines looked toward Dagon and Baal as well as other Canaanite deities for fertility and guidance. The spiritual trends observed in Israel at this time were not merely those that reflected Syncretism, but in many cases involved the total abandonment of the worship of Jehovah in favor of other national deities.

B. *The Consequences of Israel's Sin* (vv. 7-12)

While idolatry seemed attractive at first, after eighteen years of oppression and warfare, the Israelites were forced to reconsider the advantages of such commitments. Their affections, which had been directed to other gods, caused the anger of the Lord to be stirred against Israel, and as a result, God permitted them to be subject to two foreign nations: the Philistines to the southwest, and the Ammonites to the east. The awesome power of Ammon is expressed in verse 9 when it indicates that their victory marches had led them through Reuben's territory to the east of the Jordan and then up into the central hill country finally encountering the armies of Judah, Benjamin and Ephraim. Presumably, these tribes were not able to successfully stop the Ammonite penetration into central Israel. Military and spiritual frustration led Israel to cry once again to her God. With her self-confidence gone, illusive dreams of pleasure vanished, the people finally turned to the God who had been faithful to them all the time. They suddenly realized that idolatry had betrayed them and that heathen idols were entirely impotent to help them in the time of crisis. However, a mere recognition of sin was not enough this time (cf. v. 10). God wanted repentance and a total, unqualified commitment from His people that they would again obey the law.

C. *The Challenge of Jehovah* (vv. 13-14)

Before the Lord responded to their need, He gave them a very significant challenge. Since Israel had turned to the gods of Canaan and Syria and Moab and Zidon, why in times of crisis did they not look to those gods for deliverance? Verse 14 records the awesome words of God, "Go and cry unto the gods which ye have chosen; let them deliver you in the time of your tribulation." These words could not help but pierce to the very hearts of the wicked Israelites. They realized that prayers to the deities about them were of no avail at this stage. In their utter helplessness and sorrow of heart, they again turned heavenward and cried to their God.

D. *The Compassion of Jehovah* (vv. 15-18)

The greatness of Jehovah and His intense love for His people is nowhere more evident than in this particular situation. The inspired writer records the fact that as Israel cried out to their God "his soul was grieved for the misery of Israel" (v. 16). Human passion and concern would long since have been exhausted if it had encountered the kind of rebellion that Jehovah witnessed. However, God is infinite in his mercy and love, and in Israel's great distress He was grieved. His people, however, would not go without deliverance. Chapter 11 will introduce us to one of the most interesting of the judges and, we might add, one of the more problematic. The complete frustration of Israel's leaders is in evidence in verses 17, 18. As the Ammonites began to regroup their forces, now in control of most of Gilead, the princes looked one to another and found that they had no one to lead them effectively (v. 18).

III. DELIVERANCE AND FREEDOM (11:1 – 12:15)

A. *The Call of Jephthah* (11:1-11)

In the year 1089 B.C. a man appeared who seemed to have the qualifications to meet the Ammonite challenge. He was a man of strange background — a Gileadite — a man recognized for his military strength and skill, and yet rejected by his own brothers because he was a son of a harlot (v. 1). The bitterness of his brothers was so great that he was driven out of their territory, and had to dwell in the land of Tob. While in Tob, he gathered about him a small band of men and fought a number of small battles. They were in a sense soldiers of fortune, probably making their living by hiring out as mercenaries or scouts. When the elders of Israel were searching for one to lead their armies, he was requested by the elders to become their captain and their leader (vv. 5-6). This opportunity came as somewhat of a surprise to Jephthah in the light of the previous treatment accorded him (v. 7). The elders, however, were not concerned about his background or even his morality. They were interested in one thing and that was a man with military capability (v. 8). Jephthah was willing to accept this responsibility only on the condition that after a victory was achieved he would not be driven out of the land again. With this, Jephthah and the elders met together before the Lord in Mizpeh, and the agreement was concluded (vv. 9-11).

B. *Negotiations with Ammon* (11:12-29)

Jephthah's first act was not to marshal the armies of Israel together and confront the Ammonites, who at this time were enjoying unparalleled success, but rather to negotiate for peace. Messengers were sent to the king of Ammon asking what the issues really were in the conflict with Israel (v. 12). According to the king of Ammon, Israel had no legitimate right to the territory which they occupied on the east bank of Jordan. He evidently knew something of the history of Israel's conquest of the land, for he made reference to their exodus out of Egypt, and their settlement in Transjordan. His request was a simple one: Restore those lands without reservation (v. 13). Jephthah replied to the king of Ammon by pointing out that he too knew Old Testament history. He reminded the arrogant king that when Israel marched up through Edom into Moab that the territory at that time was under the control of Sihon who was king of the Amorites (vv. 16-19). Sihon refused peaceful passage through the territory, and the area was conquered by Israel.

Beginning with verse 21, Jephthah postulated four arguments in answer to the charge of the king of Ammon. First of all he pointed out that the land which Israel possessed was originally in the hands of the Amorites, not the Ammonites (cf. Num. 21:21-30; Josh. 13:25). The second argument of Jephthah was a religious argument stating that the God of Israel gave that land to Israel. Even the pagans recognized that when victory was given by a deity, the victors had full right to possess that territory. Notice verse 24, "Wilt not thou possess that which Chemosh thy god giveth thee to possess?" By way of note, we might add that Chemosh was generally regarded as the god of the Moabites; whereas, Milcom was the god of Ammon (cf. I Kings 11:5, 33). This is not an error on the part of Jephthah. He was far too familiar with the cultures east of the Jordan to make such an obvious error. The territory to which the king of Ammon was referring in this discussion was really territory originally belonging to both the Amorites and the Moabites; therefore, it was appropriate to refer to the god of that territory as Chemosh. In the famous Moabite Stone inscription the king of Moab mentioned in II Kings 3:4-5, ascribes all Moabite victories to the good will of Chemosh and all defeats to his anger. The third argument of Jephthah was one based on political precedent. He raised the question that if Balak, an earlier king of Moab, did not fight against Israel on the grounds of land rights, why then should the king of Ammon do so this late in history? It is true that Balak resisted Israel in that territory, but only because of his personal hatred of the nation, not because he was attempting to make formal claim on that territory. The final argument of Jephthah in the negotiations was a time argument.

The information provided by Jephthah in verse 26 is most instructive. He pointed out that the king of Ammon had, in effect, waited too long to make claim to that territory, for 300 years had passed since Israel dwelled in Heshbon on the east side of the Jordan. If the land did not really belong to Israel by right of conquest, then why was not the claim made to it much earlier? As noted in the introduction (cf. page 18), this statement by Jephthah is most important. It indicates that the period of the judges must cover approximately 350 years. If 144 years, representing the time from the second year of Jephthah to the fourth year of Solomon, and thirty-eight years from the Exodus to Heshbon should be added to this total, the total would be approximately 482 years which is in general agreement with the statement made in I Kings 6:1 that there were 480 years between the Exodus and the fourth year of Solomon.

The impressive arguments of Jephthah, however, were of no avail. The children of Ammon refused to end their aggression. As in the case of past judges, the Spirit of the Lord came upon Jephthah in order to give him the necessary strength and wisdom for the challenge that lay ahead (v. 29).

C. *Jephthah's Vow* (vv. 30-40)

1. *The Reason for the Vow.*

The situation which Jephthah faced was a serious and a critical one. He realized that apart from divine intervention, an engagement with the powerful Ammonite armies might spell disaster for Israel. Surrounded by tension and concern, Jephthah uttered a vow unto the Lord (v. 30). This vow required a divine response which would guarantee victory over the Ammonites.

2. *The Nature of the Vow.*

Scholars are not quite sure just how to interpret or evaluate the vow made by Jephthah. Some understand it as an act of deep piety before God. Others feel that it was rash and unfortunate. Until the middle ages the interpretation of this vow seems to have been fairly consistent. It was generally regarded as a vow toward human sacrifice. Josephus, for example, says that Jephthah "sacrificed his daughter as a burnt offering; offering such an oblation as was neither conformable to the law, nor acceptable to God, not weighing with himself what opinion the hearers would have of such a practice."[42]

In recent days, however, interpreters have presented an alternative to that view. Many feel that the vow involved mere dedication to temple service rather than sacrifice. There are, therefore, today, two prevailing interpretations of this portion of Chapter 11. The first is that he did not kill his daughter. This view is suggested by a number of conservative writers.[43] The arguments for this view are as follows: (1) Jephthah was too well acquainted with the law to be ignorant of God's condemnation of human sacrifices (cf. 11:15-27). (2) He must have known that a human being would come out of the home. Furthermore, an animal would have been too small a sacrifice for such a victory. (3) Jephthah must have been a godly man, or his name would not have appeared in Hebrews 11. (4) If his daughter were to be slain, there would be no point in emphasizing her virginity (vv. 37-39). (5) Jephthah could not have done this especially after the Spirit of God came upon him (v. 29). (6) There were women at this time who gave their lives to serving the Lord in the tabernacle at Shiloh (I Sam. 2:22; 3:19, 21. Thus, Jephthah could have vowed that in case of victory, he would dedicate to God for tabernacle service one member of his household. The fact that it turned out to be his daughter was tragic for him. Because she was his only child; he could never expect to see grandchildren; and he would seldom, if ever, see her again. (7) It is argued that the conjunction which appears in the vow in verse 31 should be translated "or" rather than "and." In other words, Jephthah is thought to have said, "Whatever comes from the doors of my home to meet me as I return shall be devoted to the Lord's service if it is human, or if it is a clean animal, I will offer it up as a whole burnt

---

[42]*Ant.* V: 7:10.

[43]C. F. Keil and F. Delitzsch, *Biblical Commentary on the Old Testament; Joshua, Judges, Ruth* (Grand Rapids: Wm. B. Eerdmans Publishing Co., 1950), p. 388 ff.

Gleason Archer, *A Survey of Old Testament Introduction* (Chicago: Moody Press, 1964), p. 266 ff.

offering." (8) It is argued by those holding this view that the
expression "to lament" in verse 40 should be translated "to
talk to" indicating that the daughter remained alive.

Briefly let us evaluate the arguments that are presented in
support of this view. First of all, even though Jephthah was
acquainted with the Pentateuch, that would not guarantee the
fact that he would not violate the law. We should recall that
David knew the law well, and yet committed adultery. The fact
that Jephthah's name appears in Hebrews 11 is not an effective
argument for the fact that he did not commit sin. In Hebrews
11, the names of Rahab and Samson also appear, and both are
known to have committed evil deeds. It is true that the Spirit
of the Lord came upon Jephthah, but we cannot be sure that
this event immediately preceded the vow which he made unto
the Lord, for it appears in verse 29 that there was a considerable amount of travel between that event and the time when
he made a vow unto the Lord. Furthermore, the fact that the
Spirit of the Lord came upon him does not guarantee that all
of his future acts would be without sin. Remember again that
Samson received the Spirit, and many of his acts were wicked.
Recall also that David was probably filled with the Spirit for
kingship, and he committed adultery. The argument that there
was a group of virgins at this time serving the Lord at the
tabernacle at Shiloh is an extremely weak one. The women referred to in I Samuel 2:22 and Exodus 38:8 are not clearly
associated with the tabernacle as *permanent residents*. Also,
there is no evidence in this text, or any other text in the Old
Testament, that women should be treated in the sense of nuns.
Perpetual virginity and childlessness were looked upon as the
greatest of misfortunes. There is no law or custom in the Old
Testament that intimates that a single woman was looked upon
as more holy than a married one. We might point out that
Deborah and Huldah were both prophetesses and were both
married. The final argument offered by the advocates of this
view is that the conjunction in verse 31 used in Jephthah's vow
should be translated "or" rather than "and." While it is true that
the Hebrew conjunction, *waw* can be used disjunctively or con-
junctively, it is extremely doubtful that the disjunctive use ("or")
is used here. It is also extremely doubtful that Jephthah had an

animal sacrifice in mind at all, for such a formal vow was quite unnecessary to bring an animal sacrifice after a great victory.

The second view with regard to Jephthah's vow and its fulfillment is that he did offer his daughter as a human sacrifice. Again this view is supported by many well-known writers.[44] The arguments for this view are as follows: (1) The Hebrew word for burnt offering is 'olāh which always has the idea of a burnt sacrifice in the Old Testament. Of particular significance is the fact that the Hebrew of 11:31 is essentially the same as that used to describe God's command to Abraham regarding the sacrifice of Isaac (Gen. 22:2). One would think that if Jephthah had dedication in mind, he would have used language similar to that which Hannah employed in the dedication of Samuel (I Sam. 1:11, 22, 25, 28). (2) Jephthah was the son of a common heathen prostitute (Zonah) and spent a great deal of time with various peoples on the east side of the Jordan (11:1-3). Furthermore, it should be observed that later individuals engaged in such human sacrifice. II Kings 3:26-27 records the action of the king of Moab in offering his eldest son for a burnt offering on the wall of his city. II Chronicles 28:3 tells of Ahaz's burning of his children, and II Kings 21:6 tells of Manasseh's sacrifice of his son. If such practices were followed by leaders in Israel at a later period, it is not impossible that they could have been introduced at this earlier period. (3) The fact that Jephthah was a judge of Israel does not remove the possibility of his making a rash vow. The dominant philosophy of this day was a moral and spiritual relativism in which "every man did that which was right in his own eyes" (Judg. 21:25). Many of Israel's leaders were affected by this attitude. Recall that Gideon made a golden ephod which led Israel to idolatry, and Samson engaged in activities that were obviously in opposition to the law of Moses. (4) If Jephthah could lead in the slaughter of 42,000 Israelites (Judg. 12), he would there-

---

[44]J. Barton Payne, *The Theology of the Older Testament* (Grand Rapids: Zondervan Publishing House, 1962), p. 388.

John Rea, "Jephthah" *The New Bible Dictionary*. J. D. Douglas (ed.) (Grand Rapids: Wm. B. Eerdmans Publishing Co., 1962), p. 605.

F. F. Bruce, "Judges" *The New Bible Commentary*. F. Davidson (ed.) (Grand Rapids: Wm. B. Eerdmans Publishing Co., 1954), p. 250.

fore be capable of this vow and its fulfillment. (5) The fact that her virginity is bewailed in verses 36-40 seems to imply that there was no hope for children in the future because of her impending death. This discussion "is probably mentioned to give greater force to the sacrifice, as it would leave him without issue, which in the east was considered a special misfortune."[45] Finally, the argument based upon the Hebrew word for "lament" in verse 40 by those holding the dedication view is rather tenuous. The verb *tanah* occurs only once elsewhere in the Hebrew Bible (Judg. 5:11). The best translation of this form appears to be "to recount."[46]

When all the evidence is weighed, it appears that the latter viewpoint is preferable, even though it is not appealing.

One question might be raised here with regard to this view, however, and that is, "If he made clear that he was going to sacrifice a human being, would God have honored that vow?" There is no doubt that Jephthah did achieve victory over the Ammonites. Space will not permit a discussion of this particular problem, but it is one which the student should consider.

D. *The Ephraimite War* (12:1-15)

1. *The Pride of Ephraim* (12:1-4)

When the Ephraimites appealed to Gideon with regard to being passed over in national affairs, they encountered a sympathetic ear (Judg. 8:1-3). However, the case was different with Jephthah. They again complained that they had not been called in the battle against the Ammonites, a claim which Jephthah refused to accept (cf. v. 2). They even threatened to destroy his house with fire (v. 1). According to Jephthah, the lack of support on the part of Ephraim put his very life in danger (v. 3). As a result, Jephthah gathered together the men of Gilead

---

[45]Merrill F. Unger, *Unger's Bible Dictionary* (Chicago: Moody Press, 1957), p. 569.

[46]Francis Brown, S. R. Driver and Charles Briggs, *A Hebrew and English Lexicon of the Old Testament* (Oxford: The Clarendon Press, Corrected Impression, 1952), p. 1072.

and fought with the Ephraimites. The cause of warfare, however, was much greater than a personal feud between Jephthah and the men of Ephraim. Verse 4 indicates that the Gileadites had developed a hatred for the Ephraimites and the Manassites living on the west side of the Jordan. Why a jealousy arose between the Manassites on the east of the Jordan and those on the west is not given to us in the text. But this attitude, coupled with the impatience of Jephthah, led to the intertribal war which spelled disaster for the tribe of Ephraim.

2. *Encounter and Defeat* (vv. 5-7)

When the war broke out between Ephraim and the Gileadites, the Gileadites secured positions along the Jordan River, thereby preventing the escape of the Ephraimites back to the west. Anyone who attempted to cross the Jordan at this time would have been stopped by the Gileadite soldiers and asked to pronounce a special password. The word that was required was "shibboleth." Evidently some type of dialectical differences had developed between the Gileadites and the tribes on the west bank. The Ephraimite pronunciation of this word might constitute what was commonly called an isogloss (a linguistic phenomenon characteristic of a given area). It is rather strange that the Ephraimites were incapable of pronouncing a sibilant which was common to all west Semitic languages. E. A. Speiser suggests that the Gileadites may have pronounced the word *tubbultu* after a cognate Aramaic form.[47] In any event, according to the Hebrew text they were required to pronounce the word "shibboleth," but if they were from the west bank they would say it "sibboleth," for they were not capable of pronouncing it after the Gileadite fashion. This screening process resulted in the death of 42,000 men (v. 6). After this war, the life of Jephthah came to an end, concluding a judgeship of six years. He was buried in one of the cities of Gilead (v. 7). Thus the Biblical description of one of the most unusual judges ends. His life was one of mystery and contradiction.

---

[47]E. A. Speiser, "The Shibboleth Incident, Judges 12:6" *Bulletin of the American Schools of Oriental Research* No. 85 (Feb., 1942).

E. *Jephthah's Successors* (vv. 8-15)

1. *The Judgeship of Ibzan* (vv. 8-10)

This judge ruled in Israel for a period of seven years (v. 9).
The place of his birth and residence is not clear. It is described as Bethlehem which may have been Bethlehem of Judah, or it might have reference to the Bethlehem in the tribe
of Zebulun, the present *Beit-lahm,* seven miles northwest of
Nazareth (cf. Josh. 19:15-16). He probably began his judgeship
about 1081 B.C. and this would have lasted until approximately
1075 B.C. He undoubtedly engaged in polygamous practices
and it appears that it was his policy to create marriage relation-
ships with families throughout Israel. This was probably done
to improve civil and political influence in various areas.

2. *The Judgeship of Elon* (vv. 11-12)

Following the rule of Ibzan, Elon a Zebulunite judged Israel.
According to verse 11, the judgeship lasted for ten years (1075
B.C.-1065 B.C.). Nothing else is known of this judge other
than the fact that he was buried in Aijalon in the territory of
Zebulun.

3. *The Judgeship of Abdon* (vv. 13-15)

Beginning in the year 1065 B.C. Abdon became the principal
judge in Israel. He remained judge for approximately eight
years (v. 14). According to the information in verse 15, he
probably was an Ephraimite. He evidently had achieved wide
acclaim for his rather large family which included forty sons
and thirty grandsons, all of which rode on ass colts — a sign of
prestige and authority (cf. 10:4). According to verse 15, he
was buried in Pirathon in the land of Ephraim, which evidently
was occupied by the Amalekites during this period of time.

IV. PRACTICAL CONSIDERATIONS

This portion of Scripture gives us interesting insights into the
character and power of God as well as the weakness and
failures of men. God is seen as sensitive and compassionate with
regard to the needs of His people in spite of their constant

rebellion against Him (10:16). One cannot help but be impressed with the infinite patience of God. Time and time again Israel turned her back on the very Lord who had provided for her and redeemed her. These Scriptures re-emphasize the fact that while Jehovah has a deep hatred for sin, He at the same time has an unending compassion for the sinner.

The power of God is also a dominant theme in this section of Scripture. Not only was the Lord sensitive and compassionate to the needs of Israel, but He had the necessary power at His disposal to meet those needs, even if it meant utilizing weak and frail men. The men described in this section of Judges were indeed weak and in many cases undependable. Certainly the victory and the freedom brought to Israel during this period was not the result of human achievement alone. God delivered His people in spite of the weakness of the leaders He had to use. This indeed is an encouragement. It reminds us that the purposes of God cannot be frustrated either by the designs of Satan or the weaknesses of men. The believer is again reminded that nothing short of a thorough knowledge of the Word of God and obedience to it will suffice in the conflicts which he will encounter.

Chapter 10

SAMSON — MAN OF STRENGTH
(Judges 13–16)

Beginning with the twelfth century the Philistines began to play a dominant role in politics and the military affairs of the land of Canaan. This was no accident in history, for Judges 13 records the fact that Israel again did evil in the sight of the Lord. We might assume that there was a return to the kind of idolatry described in the previous chapters. Because of this situation, God permitted the Philistines to strengthen themselves and for forty years to dominate Israel (13:1).

Prior to the time of Samson, the Philistines had played a small, but significant, role in the historical developments of southern Palestine (cf. 3:31; 10:7-11). When Ramses III turned back the invasion of sea peoples in 1194 B.C., this caused many Philistines to settle the coast lands of southwest Palestine. They joined the earlier Minoan settlers and became a significant military force in the years that followed. The judgeship of Samson began about 1069 B.C. and continued until about 1049 B.C. The historical information provided by the monuments of Ramses III help to provide the cultural and military background for the events in the time of Samson.

I. THE BIRTH OF SAMSON (13:2-25)

A. *His Family* (v. 1)

The parents of Samson resided in a border city (Zorah) between Dan and Judah, approximately seventeen miles west of Jerusalem. Manoah and his wife had not been blessed with a child, which was considered a great calamity to a Hebrew woman. The same tragedy was ascribed to Sarai (Gen. 16:1), Rebekah (Gen. 25:21), Hannah (I Sam. 1:2), and Elizabeth (Luke 1:7). God, in His providence and omniscience, looked to the day when Israel would require deliverance and an outstanding leader. Manoah and his wife were to be part of God's plan.

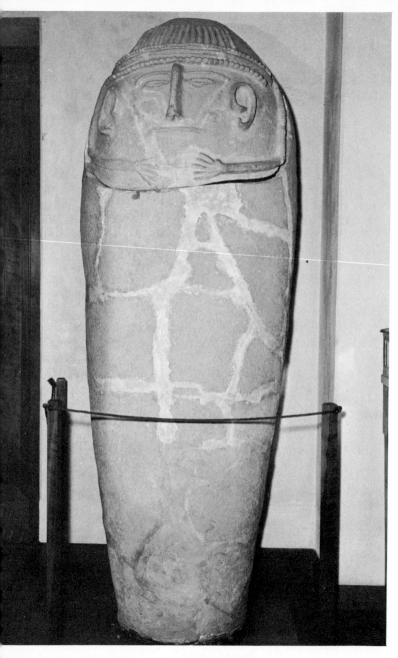

Philistine Anthropoid Coffin. Levant Photo Service

B. *The Announcement of His Birth* (vv. 3-23)

The announcement of the birth of a child is not without parallel elsewhere in Scripture. Isaac's birth was announced as was John the Baptist's and the Lord Jesus'. The announcement of the birth was brought by the angel of Jehovah, who had appeared previously to Gideon and others during the period of the Judges. The initial appearance of the angel of the Lord was only to the wife of Manoah. On that occasion, she was informed that she would conceive and bear a son (v. 3). In addition to that, it was made clear that this child was to be a Nazarite unto God (v. 5). According to Numbers 6:1-6, the Nazarite had three restrictions placed upon him: (1) He was to abstain from wine (Num. 6:3-4). (2) He was to allow the hair of his head to go untouched by a razor (Num. 6:5). (3) He was not to touch a dead body in order that he might prevent defilement (Num. 6:6).

Following this conversation, the wife of Manoah came to him and brought the news which had been given to her by the angel of the Lord. Manoah's response is most impressive and instructive. He did not question the message brought to his wife, but sought further instructions. He requested another appearance of the man of God in order to receive instruction on rearing the child. That prayer was answered by God (v. 9). Once again the man of God appeared — this time to both of them — and Manoah's principal concerns were repeated. They took the form of two questions. The first one literally translated is "What shall be the ordering of the child?"; that is, "What shall be the rule of life for this child?" He then asked, "What shall be his work?" (v. 12). Manoah was searching for confirmation of the original message given to his wife and additional instruction as to their responsibility in rearing the child. Up to this point Manoah did not realize that he stood face to face with the angel of the Lord (v. 16). He inquired further of the identity of this visitor by asking his name (v. 17). The angel responded by saying, "Why askest thou thus after my name, seeing it is secret?" (v. 18). The last word of this sentence might better be translated "wonderful" (Heb. *peli'y*). This is the same word that occurs in Isaiah 9:5 and is rendered "won-

derful" (cf. 13:19, "wondrously"). After a special offering was
miraculously consumed by fire and the angel of the Lord ascend-
ed in the flame heavenward, Manoah immediately knew that it
was the angel of the Lord (v. 21). He, like Gideon, was struck
by great fear because he thought he had seen God and would
therefore die (cf. Judg. 6:23; Exod. 33:20). His wife assured
him that he would not die for this was certainly not God's will
in this case (v. 23).

C. *His Birth* (vv. 24-25)

In the fullness of time, Samson was born and the Lord blessed
him (v. 24). There has been some speculation as to what the
name of Samson means. It most likely comes from the Hebrew
Šemeš which means "sun." Some suggest, on this basis, that
it has the idea of "brightness." We are not informed as to what
happened in the childhood days of Samson. Verse 25 merely
indicates that the Spirit of Jehovah moved him at times in the
camp of Dan between Zorah and Eshtaol.

II. THE MARRIAGE OF SAMSON (14:1-20)

A. *The Woman in Timnath* (vv. 1-4)

Because of the proximity of the tribe of Dan to the center
of Philistine influence, it was not surprising that Samson came
in contact with a number of the young ladies from Philistia.
According to verses 1-4, he was very much attracted to one of
the women among the daughters of the Philistines. In order to
make arrangements for his marriage he came to his mother and
father. His parents, of course, knowing the law and having a
commitment to the spiritual future of Samson, immediately objected to this kind of arrangement. The ultimate concerns of
Samson in this case were not spiritual, but personal; "Get her
for me; for she pleaseth me well" (v. 3). The parents of Samson
did not realize that even this evil act on the part of their son
was included in, and would be utilized by, God in His perfect
plan. The writer of the text looked back over the history of
Samson and saw in his movements, and even in his weaknesses,
the hand of God. The marriage between Samson and a Philistine

woman ultimately resulted in the destruction of many of Israel's enemies. Verse 4 points to the fact that "he sought an occasion against the Philistines." The antecedent of "he" is probably Jehovah, although grammatically it could refer to Samson as well. In view of the theological nature of the first statement of this verse, it appears that Jehovah is meant, rather than Samson.

B. *The Lion and the Riddle* (vv. 5-20)

Evidently, Samson persisted in his demands to take the young girl from Timnath as his wife. His father and mother proceeded to Timnath to make the necessary arrangements for the marriage (v. 5). Later Samson made the trip in that direction and on the way he was encountered by a young lion, one in the prime of life (Heb. *kepîr*). The Spirit of the Lord came upon him (v. 6), giving him the necessary strength and skill to slay that lion. After having visited his prospective wife, he went back to his home (v. 7). Later he returned to Timnath to "take her" (v. 8), and on the way he noticed the dry, clean carcass (skeleton?) of the lion which he had slain. A swarm of bees had produced honey in that carcass so he stopped to eat and enjoy it. Bees, of course, avoid any kind of decomposition. We probably should assume here that birds and decay had cleared away all of the decayed material, leaving a skeleton. Again, Samson kept this event a secret (v. 9). After the wedding a feast was prepared for Samson and his bride (v. 10). The Hebrew of this verse is very important, for this was no mere "feast." The Hebrew indicates that this was a "drinking feast" (Heb. *mišteh*). Thus, in a short period of time Samson had violated two of the requirements for the Nazarite. He had contaminated himself ceremonially by touching the carcass of the lion, and he had participated in a drinking feast.

His future was further complicated when, according to local customs, he told a riddle (v. 12). The pride of those gathered there would not permit them to admit they could not analyze the riddle or interpret it. Finally, on the seventh day of the feast week, they came to Samson's wife and demanded the answer to the riddle, on the threat that they would burn her house (v. 15). The men were able to go back to Samson and explain the riddle to him (v. 18). He recognized the source of their information, but nonetheless paid off the obligation he had to these men.

It might be noted, however, that he paid off his debt at their expense. Again, the Spirit of the Lord came upon him (v. 19), and he went down to Ashkelon, an important Philistine city. There he slew thirty men, and took their garments to pay off the men who had explained the riddle. In the meantime, however, the father-in-law was convinced that Samson was irresponsible and really unconcerned for this young girl from Timnath; thus, in the process of time she was given to the best man. This complicated the life of Samson even further (v. 20), but not without divine purpose (cf. 14:4).

III. SAMSON AND THE PHILISTINES (15:1-16:31)

A. *The Rise of Samson to Power* (15:1-20)

The Return to Timnath (15:1-13)

A short time after the wedding feast, Samson returned to Timnath to get his wife. He evidently did not see his wife after he went to Ashkelon and now it was the time of the wheat harvest, or about the middle of May. His father-in-law had already taken steps to find another husband for his daughter (vv. 1-2). He did, however, offer Samson his younger daughter who, he claimed was even fairer than she (v. 2). This proposition, interestingly enough, has a familiar ring to it (cf. Gen. 29:17 ff.). Samson, very displeased with this situation, again turned against the Philistines, resulting in the destruction of many of their crops. He caught some three hundred jackals (v. 4), tied torches between their tails, and set them free in the grain fields of the Philistines (v. 5). When the Philistines witnessed this mass destruction of their crops, they revenged this act by burning the house of Samson's father-in-law (v. 6). It is ironic that this house should be destroyed by fire, for earlier the wife of Samson attempted to save the house from such a fate by betraying the trust of Samson (14:15). This act on the part of the Philistines enraged Samson further. According to the principle of *Lex Taliones* Samson dealt with the Philistines in violence once again. This time "he smote them hip and thigh with a great slaughter" (v. 8). The idiom "hip and thigh" is simply a proverbial expression for "completely" or "entirely." The Philistines then responded to this by going up into Judah in order to take Samson captive (v. 9). The men of Judah at this time were very weak and not in a position to resist the Philistines or to reject their demands. Three thousand men of Judah went to Samson, which indicated their great respect for his strength (v. 11). When they inquired of Samson why he had acted the way he did in increasing the belligerency of the Philistines, he merely responded that he had treated them just as they had treated him (v. 11). They took Samson and bound him with two "new cords" (v. 13), but these were not to last, for the Spirit of God came upon him again (v. 14), and the cords were broken. On this occasion he slaughtered one thousand men (v. 15). This was accomplished with a fresh or moist jawbone of an ass. It is not impossible that Samson was assisted by the men of Judah on this occasion, although he took full credit for the victory (v. 16). His arrogance and self-sufficiency were not overlooked by the Lord. In physical thirst and weakness, he was forced to call on the Lord. The Lord heard that cry and strengthened him (vv. 18-20).

B. *The Fall of Samson into Sin* (16:1-22)

1. *Samson at Gaza* (vv. 1-3)

While Samson had control of his great power, he unfortunately did not have the same control over his passions. At Gaza he spent time with a harlot and this situation again brought him into great danger. The men of the city heard of his presence there and surrounded the city, waiting for morning to come when they could initiate a detailed search to locate him (v. 2). However, when Samson rose at midnight and prepared to leave the city, he found that all the gates were shut tight. This, of course, was no problem to a man of Samson's strength. He merely tore the gates from their posts and carried them toward Hebron! Since Hebron is approximately thirty miles from Gaza, it is doubtful that he carried them all the way to the city. The Hebrew seems to imply that he carried them to the foothills which are before Hebron.

2. *Samson and Delilah* (vv. 4-22)

Sometime after his escape from Gaza, he found a woman in the valley of Sorek. Samson had spent much of his life in this

valley — now known as Wadi es-Surar — which starts about
fifteen miles west of Jerusalem and runs toward the coastal
plain. The town of Zorah, Samson's home, was situated in this
valley. The name of the woman whom he loved was Delilah.
No other information is given about her in the Scriptures. Many
have supposed she was a Philistine, but this is merely an assumption. It is not clearly indicated as to whether she became his
wife or not. In all probability, she was not, in the light of
his previous activities as described in verses 1 through 3.
In any event, the lords of the Philistine Pentapolis (Heb. *sarnê
pelištîm*) offered 5,500 pieces of silver for the secret of Samson's
strength (v. 5).

Delilah then set out to discover that secret. Samson responded
to her questions in an arrogant, playful attitude. He first told
her that if he were bound with seven green (Heb. "moist")
ropes or bow strings that were never dried, he would be as
another man (v. 7). This she did, and then called in Philistine soldiers to take him prisoner. Using his strength, he broke
these and presumably killed the men. This, of course, displeased
Delilah greatly (v. 10), and why should it not? Five thousand
five hundred pieces of silver were at stake here! Again she
pressed him for the secret of his strength, and again he gave her
false information. This time he suggested "new ropes" should
be used and he would then be as any other man (v. 11). She
then called the Philistine soldiers, and again the cords were
broken (v. 12). This situation was becoming costly to the
Philistine lords and embarrassing to Delilah. She reprimanded
Samson for his deceit and mockery, and once again sought the
secret of his strength (v. 13). In arrogant pride he continued to
play the game with her. He suggested that if seven locks of his
hair were woven into a web, he would be helpless; so she
began to weave the hair, and when he had fallen asleep, she
called for the Philistine soldiers. Once again he tore loose from
the weaver's beam and presumably slew the men waiting to take
him prisoner (v. 14). This was indeed a frustration for Delilah.
The silver was so close and yet so far! But she did not end her
search at this point. Verse 16 informs us that she pressed him
daily, questioning and taunting him concerning his strength, until
finally he revealed his secret. He pointed to the fact that he

was dedicated as a Nazarite to God and if he were shaven, his strength would leave him (vv. 16-17). There was no doubt in Delilah's mind this time that he had spoken the truth (v. 18).

The scene that follows is tragic and one of the darkest moments in the history of the Judges. Delilah called for the Philistine lords and instructed them to bring the silver which they had promised (v. 18). After Samson had fallen asleep, his head was shaven, and when awakened, he was unable to defend himself as he had in the past (vv. 18-20). It was not the mere loss of hair that brought Samson into humiliation; it was his disobedience to God and the complete violation of the Nazarite vow. The pride and insensitivity of Samson is clearly viewed in verse 20. He assumed that he would go out as before and care for the threat of the Philistines, but he did not know that Jehovah — that is, the strength of Jehovah — had departed from him. Like many believers, Samson was asleep when he lost his strength. To add to the humiliation, the Philistines took him captive, put out his eyes, and took him down to Gaza, the city which he had left so arrogantly by destroying their gates. They bound him with fetters of bronze and took him to the prison house where he worked as an animal (v. 21). The down-fall of Samson was not due to a failure on God's part, but it was due to Samson's uncontrolled pride and sinful passion.

C. The Death of Samson (16:23-31)

The humiliation of Samson did not end with his imprisonment or the removal of his eyes. Later he was taken to the temple dedicated to the Philistine god, Dagon (vv. 23-24). The term Dagon has been traced to two Hebrew roots. One suggestion is that it comes from *dāg*, meaning "fish." Supporting this theory are a number of coins found at Ashkelon, having an image of a deity that was half man and half fish. A preferred view, however, traces the term to *dāgān*, which means "grain." If this is the case, Dagon would be a fertility god. In Ugaritic literature Baal is referred to as the "son of Dagon." This deity was evidently recognized widely in the land of Caanan, especially along the coast. The capture and humiliation of Samson was the cause of great rejoicing in the cities of Philistia (vv. 23-24). In order to make the most of their capture of Samson, they brought him to the temple of Dagon, where, now blind and in chains, he was the object of laughter and scorn. This was also an occasion of praise and thanksgiving to the gods of the Philistines (v. 25).

This temple must have been of considerable size. It probably had a long main hall with adjacent rooms. The complex was capable of supporting approximately three thousand men and women on the roof as well as a large number inside the temple complex (v. 27). While voices were lifted in praise to Dagon, Samson also lifted his voice. For the first time in years, he realized he had to throw himself on the mercy of God and depend on His help. In utter simplicity Samson prayed to his God. The essence of his prayer is wrapped up in two key words: "Remember me" (v. 28). This kind of prayer is indicative of a soul in need. Two other times in Biblical history a similar prayer was offered. Hannah, in a state of despair and frustration, came to the tabernacle and lifted up her voice in prayer to her God. In bitterness of soul she cried to heaven, "Remember me" (I Sam. 1: 11). The Lord recognized the sincerity of this prayer and answered it by giving her a child, Samuel. Many years later, a similar prayer was offered. This time it was at Calvary. One of the malefactors who was hanged with Jesus looked at him with faith and said, "Lord *remember me* when thou comest into thy kingdom" (Luke 23:42). Again, the Lord recognized the sincerity and simplicity of that request. To it He replied, "Today shalt thou be with me in paradise" (Luke 23:43). The Lord likewise recognized the sincerity of Samson's plea and answered his prayer, giving to him strength, enough strength to destroy the temple of the Philistines and those gathered inside (vv. 29-31). This last heroic act brought an end to his life.

IV. PRACTICAL CONSIDERATIONS

The life of Samson is a study in contrasts. There was the godliness and sensitiveness of his parents. In contrast to this was the arrogance and self-sufficiency of Samson. Samson was a man of great gifts, and yet a man who failed to utilize them to the greatest degree in bringing glory to his God. Samson realized many victories and yet suffered many losses. While Samson was

Chapter 11

CONFUSION AND CONFLICT
(Judges 17–21)

The last five chapters of this book represent the author's supplement or appendix to the history of the Judges period. The author intended to provide further insight into the issues which gave rise to the conflicts of this and later periods. The history of this period is dealt with in the local sense as it related to families and clans and, of course, as related to Israel as a nation. As was the case in the earlier chapters of the Book of Judges, these chapters deal with the subject of spiritual apostasy and its effects upon the nation of Israel.

I. THE DANITE MIGRATION (17:1–18:31)

A. *The Idolatry of Micah* (17:1-13)

A careful reader of this chapter will find important instruction with regard to the nature and effects of apostasy as it is viewed in the life of one individual and his family. The apostasy of the Judges period, according to this chapter, was characterized by three observable trends.

1. *Religious Syncretism* (17:1-5)

Religious syncretism involves the blending together of different religious attitudes and ideas into one system. This trend was observable in the lives of Micah and his family as they were affected by the popular trends of their day. According to verse 1, Micah was an Ephramite. This fact is significant because the tabernacle was set up at Shiloh which is in Ephraimite territory. However, as we study the story of Micah, it becomes clear that Shiloh had lost its spiritual influence among many of the families and clans within the tribe of Ephraim. If this were the case for the tribe of Ephraim, how much less influence must the sanctuary at Shiloh have had among the other tribes located in more distant regions? In spite of the significance of Micah's name ("who is as Jehovah?") it is clear that he was very much caught up with the spirit of his generation. He had gone so far as to

143

steal from his mother. According to verse 2, he had taken eleven hundred shekels of silver. This, as we learn from 16:5, was no small amount. When the money was taken, his mother had evidently put a curse upon the thief, and as time went on, Micah found himself unable to use the silver because of the curse. He therefore returned the money to his mother and she responded with praise (v. 2). This theft on the part of Micah was probably characteristic of his age. When the law was abandoned and its principles forsaken, dishonesty and thievery probably characterized everyday life in Israel (cf. 18:14-19). Following the return of the money, the mother indicated that she had "wholly dedicated this silver to Jehovah" (v. 3).

Again it appears we have a normal religious situation. However, two hundred shekels of silver were used by that mother and Micah to make a "graven image" and "molten image" (v. 4). The religious syncretism of this period is clearly illustrated in these verses. Money which was "dedicated to Jehovah" was, in effect, to be employed for the making of idols. It is entirely possible that these idols were in some way used in the worship of Jehovah, thus reflecting the blending together of Canaanite cultic practices and traditional worship of Jehovah. It is not clear from verse 4 whether one or two images were made from the allotted amount of silver. Some feel the second expression is merely an explanation or further description of the first. However, in 18:17, the two words are separated in such a manner as to indicate the existence of two idols. The making of the two idols was not the beginning of idolatry in Micah's household. According to verse 5, he already had a "house of gods" (Heb. *bêt 'elohîm*). In addition to this he made an ephod and used it for cultic purposes (cf. Judg. 8:27). The teraphim mentioned in verse 5 are usually interpreted as referring to household idols (Gen. 31:19, 34). They were, on occasion, used as oracular instruments (Ezek. 21:21; Zech. 10:2). It appears that some of the teraphim were rather large, perhaps having human form (cf. I Sam. 19:13-17). Worship at this site was conducted by one of his sons who became "his priest" (v. 5).

2. *Moral Relativism* (17:6)

The writer again reminds us that we are in the pre-monarchial period, for there was no "king in Israel" (cf. 18:1; 19:1; 21:25). When men began to reject the law of Moses as the standard of conduct, there was only one other way which moral activity could be conducted and that was on the basis of subjective norms; that is, every man established principles of righteousness on the basis of his own evaluation. This type of philosophy led to confusion and spiritual conflict among the tribes.

3. *Extreme Materialism* (17:7-13)

Another individual entered the scene at this point of the story who was described as a Levite from Bethlehem-judah (v. 7). His journey northward was intended to provide for him "a place" (i.e., a place of service, v. 8). Evidently this Levite was unemployed and had no place of permanent service. During his travels northward he encountered Micah who asked of him the reason for such a journey (v. 9). The Levite responded by indicating that he sought a place of service. The very fact that the Levite wandered, seeking a means of support, might indicate that the apostasy had left the Levites without tribal support. In any event, Micah extended to this young priest an official "call" to his local shrine. This included a salary of ten shekels of silver, a suit of apparel, and food (v. 10). The introduction of the Levite into this story was important because it indicated that apostasy had not only influenced the thinking of the Israelites generally, but also of the Levites and the spiritual leaders in Israel. The Levite was content to accept such a position (v. 11) in spite of what he knew of the law of Moses and its prohibitions with regard to idolatry. He was consecrated by Micah and then served as a private priest in this household (v. 12). The sinfulness of the Levite contributed to the deepening of Micah's apostasy. Now Micah became arrogant and self-sufficient in spiritual attitude for he proclaimed, "Now know I that the Lord will do me good seeing I have a Levite to my priest" (v. 13).

B. *Danite Unrest* (18:1-29)

In spite of the fact that the tribe of Dan had a military potential of 64,000 men (Num. 26:43), they were unable to occupy the territory that was allotted to them. The reason for their frustration and their interest in other territory (v. 1) is given in 1:34, of this book. According to the historian's observation, the Amorites had forced the Danites up into the mountains not permitting them to occupy the larger valleys.

Preparations for a Move (18:1-26)

Because of the problems the Danites faced they sent a spy contingent northward to search out new territories in which they could dwell safely. In the process of their journey they encountered the young Levite. According to verse 3, they knew him. Perhaps they knew him before their journey or they may have recognized him as a Levite by his dress. In any event, they sought special counsel from this Levite (v. 5) which he gladly gave them (v. 6). He endorsed their plan and encouraged them to seek new territory. The five men then traveled northward to a site named Laish (v. 7), elsewhere called Leshem (Josh. 19: 47). The spies noted that Laish was a peaceful town and far enough removed from the Phoenicians and Sidon as to not face another military threat. After they returned back to Philistine territory, 600 warriors with their families joined in the migration northward (vv. 11-14). Once again they passed the sanctuary of Micah, and on that day they helped themselves to the images and idols that were inside the sanctuary (v. 14). As previously noted, robbery was very common during this period (cf. 17:2-3). In addition to taking the idols of the sanctuary, they decided to give another "call" to this young priest. This time they encouraged him that his ministry would be far more effective among a whole tribe than just to a small family (v. 19). The young Levite found this offer very attractive and, therefore, joined the Danites on their trip northward. Again we are able to see the materialistic attitude of the Levite during this time.

When Micah returned home, he was much disturbed by the absence of both the objects of the sanctuary and his private "pastor." He, along with some others, pursued the Danites in an attempt to rescue his gods and his priest. When he caught up with the Danites, he explained why he had made such a journey.

His words are very enlightening, for they reflect the theological thinking of this man. First of all, in verse 24 he indicated the gods which he had made had been taken. It is rather sad that an Israelite should assume he could actually make a god. Furthermore, it was quite strange that a man should have to rescue his god. It ought to be the other way around; namely, his god providing deliverance for him. The apostasy of Micah is further illustrated by his total frustration in the light of these events, for with his idols gone and his priest gone, he said, "What have I more?" (v. 24). The Danites were not impressed by the arguments or the pleas of Micah. He was therefore forced to return home without the things which he had lost. The Danites and the young Levite priest continued their way northward to Laish and occupied that site (vv. 27-29). At that time the name of the city was changed from Laish to Dan (v. 29). Since the site is called Dan in 5:17, it is probable that the events here described occurred before the war with Sisera.

C. *Danite Idolatry* (18:30-31)

After Laish was conquered, the Danites established a sanctuary for the idols. Jonathan became the high priest at that place (v. 30). According to this verse, he was a descendant of Manasseh. It is clear from the original text that this expression should be read "the son of Moses" rather than "the son of Manasseh." A scribe evidently tried to remove the name of Moses from being associated with idolatrous practices. This verse indicates that the events described in Chapters 17 and 18 actually occurred early in the Judges period, for Jonathan is a near descendant of Moses. The "captivity of the land" referred to in this verse has been variously interpreted. Some feel it refers to the deportation of northern peoples by Tiglath-pileser (II Kings 15:29). Others feel it describes the exile of the ark from Shiloh (I Sam. 4:11) or the time of Philistine domination (I Sam. 4). The later view seems more probable in the light of the fact that the house of God at Shiloh was destroyed by the Philistines (cf. v. 31 with I Sam. 4:4). From this time onward, the city of Dan became a center of idolatry. Some years later, Jeroboam set up golden calves at Bethel and Dan (I Kings 12:29).

II. THE BENJAMITE WAR (19:1—21:25)

A. *The Reason for the War* (19:1—20:14)

Chapters 17 and 18 gave us insight into the effects of apostasy as it related to a family and a tribe. The chapter that lies before us will be a detailed analysis of the effects of apostasy among the whole nation of Israel. Perhaps most significant is the influence of idolatry and moral relativism on the tribe of Benjamin.

1. *The Crime at Gibeah* (19:1-28)

The historian begins his narrative by providing historical context for the events that are to follow. The period is the pre-monarchial era. The story again revolves around a Levite who had taken a concubine from Bethlehem-judah as a wife. In the process of time, she had become unfaithful to him resulting in a separation and her return to her father's house (vv. 1-2). The Levite then made a journey to the home of the concubine in order to restore his relationship with her. After abiding in the father-in-law's house for three days, he decided to return home, but the father-in-law insisted that he remain one more day, and this he did (vv. 5-7). On the fifth day, a similar request was made by the concubine's father, but the Levite and his wife began their journey (vv. 7-9).

Their journey northward was an eventful one. They were not able to stay in Jerusalem because it was still in the hands of the enemy (v. 12). The name of Jerusalem at that time was Jebus (v. 10), apparently named after the people who ruled it, the Jebusites (cf. I Chron. 11:4; Judg. 1:21; Josh. 18:16, 28). Because it was not safe to reside in Jerusalem, it was decided to continue northward either to Gibeah or to Ramah (v. 13). They ultimately reached Gibeah which was located in the tribal territory of Benjamin (v. 14). After entering the gate, they remained in the public square just inside the gate hoping to receive an invitation for lodging (v. 15), but such an invitation did not come. The absence of hospitality on the part of the Benjamites should be regarded as an outward sign of apostasy, for in the Old Testament a godly man, among other things, was one who extended hospitality to those in need (cf. Job 31:32).

Finally, an Ephraimite, who was sojourning in Gibeah, gave them a place to stay. During the evening certain "sons of Belial" came to the house desiring carnal relations with the Levite (v. 22).

The use of the expression "sons of Belial" is significant. This term is reserved for those who have no regard for law or morality. The term literally translated means "sons of no profit" or "sons of worthlessness." Elsewhere in the Old Testament this expression is used to describe those involved in idolatry (Deut. 13:13), rebellion (I Sam. 2:12), and drunkenness (I Sam. 1:16, here the expression is "daughter of Belial"). In this chapter it has reference to lewd and sensuous men (cf. 20:13). The story recorded here is reminiscent of the one in Genesis 19. In similar fashion, the master of the house did not give the guest to these men, but the concubine (vv. 24-25). The concubine of the Levite was then taken and abused all evening, resulting in her death (vv. 27-28). When the Levite witnessed this, he took her body home and dismembered it into twelve parts. One part of her body was sent to each tribe as a challenge and warning (vv. 29-30). The purpose of this act was to awaken Israel from its state of moral lethargy and to marshal the tribes together to face up to their responsibility. A similar deed was performed by King Saul some years later, probably to achieve the same effect (I Sam. 11:7). This act on the part of the Levite was designed to get action and it worked.

2. Responses to the Crime (20:1-14)

a. The Levite

The response of the Levite was described in the last two verses of the previous chapter. It was a response of indignation because of the open sin of the wicked men of Gibeah. The Levite felt that nothing short of immediate judgment and punishment would be satisfactory.

b. The Tribes (vv. 1-12)

When word was received regarding the crime that had been committed in Gibeah, the tribes gathered together and their armies made ready. They numbered 400,000 (v. 2). For the first time in many years the tribes were gathered together in singleness of purpose (cf. vv. 8, 11). They all agreed that the guilty party at Gibeah should be punished. Lots were cast in order to determine who should care for the food supplies for the armies (v. 10). A select group of men then went through the territory of Benjamin demanding the punishment of the guilty parties at Gibeah. The death penalty for this crime was clearly in mind (v. 13). Because of the apostasy of the tribe of Benjamin, rather than turning the guilty men over for punishment, they protected them (v. 13). They elected to go to war with the other tribes rather than have the evil men punished. Besides the 700 men from the town of Gibeah, they marshaled together 26,000 soldiers (v. 15). Among the 26,000 there were 700 left-handed men who were experts with the sling-shot (v. 16, cf. 3:15). The tension which developed during this time was probably only paralleled during the tribal conflict recorded in Joshua 22.

That the decision to fight Benjamin was not an easy one is indicated by their journey to the house of God in search of God's will (v. 18). The Lord required that Judah should go into battle first (cf. 1:3 ff.). Judah was most likely selected because of its size and fighting capability. The first battle was fought at Gibeah (v. 20) and resulted in the loss of 22,000 Israelites (v. 21). Again the leaders of Israel came before the Lord in search of His will (v. 23). The second day the tribes went to battle, and as in the previous encounter the Benjamites were successful. Eighteen thousand Israelites were slain in that battle (v. 25). This caused the tribes to again appear before God in humility and concern (vv. 26-27). Phinehas, the son of Eleazar, took the responsibility of giving guidance (v. 28). Phinehas, of course, is well known from the days of Joshua. It was he who mediated the tribal conflict described in Joshua 22. The mention of his name in this account indicates that the events here recorded must have occurred early in the Judges period.

The third battle fought between Benjamin and the other tribes was quite different from the first two. This time Israel set an ambush much like the one used by Joshua in the battle of Ai (Josh. 8:4-29). The arrogant Benjamites were drawn away from the city and then those lying in wait on the other side of the city entered the city, destroying all. This was the beginning of what was almost total annihilation for the tribe of Benjamin. When the dust of battle had settled, only 600 Benjamite males remained. These had fled to the rock of Rimmon about four miles east of Bethel (vv. 34-47).

It might be asked at this point, "Why didn't Jehovah give victory to the armies of Israel in the first two battles? Why did they suffer the loss of over 40,000 men before they realized victory?" This question, of course, is difficult to answer. It is apparent that the setbacks did have a healthy affect on the spiritual outlook of the tribes. They were driven to fasting and prayer with an earnest attempt to find the will of God.

B. *The Results of the War* (21:1-25)

The tragedy of the Benjamite war was not only in the fact that this tribe had been nearly annihilated, but that the other tribes had taken an oath not to permit the marriage of any of their daughters to a Benjamite (v. 1). The results of their victory, coupled with the oath that they had taken, meant that Benjamin might not survive as a tribe in Israel (v. 3). Their only hope for the survival of the tribe of Benjamin would be to find wives for the 600 men who remained. A search of the war records indicated that the men from Jabesh-gilead did not participate in the recent battles, and it was decided that the city should be judged (vv. 5-6). Twelve thousand soldiers were sent from the tribes to go against the city of Jabesh-gilead with the instructions to kill every man, woman, and child with the exception of the virgins (vv. 11-12). The 400 virgins were given to the surviving Benjamites, leaving only 200 without wives (v. 12). Some of the Benjamites most likely returned to Jabesh-gilead to settle down, which probably had something to do with later action on the part of Saul (a Benjamite) on behalf of that city (I Sam. 11:1 ff.). The tribes apparently felt that the provision of 400 wives was not sufficient to guarantee the surivial of Benjamin. The remaining 200 Benjamites were encouraged to "take" wives from among the maidens who danced during the festivals at Shiloh (vv. 19-21). If any of the relatives objected to this procedure, they were reminded that elders had agreed that the

Benjamites should have wives. Also, they had not, in effect, "given" these girls in marriage to the Benjamites, hence there was no violation of their oath (v. 22).

The Book of Judges concludes with a fitting evaluation of that age. The statement in verse 25 indicates both the political and moral status of Israel during that time.

Conclusion

The study of the books of Joshua and Judges is a study in contrasts. Joshua portrays the excitement of conquest and the thrill of victory. The people of God were sensitive to their covenant relationship and attempted to remain faithful to it. After the death of Joshua, the political and spiritual trends in Israel changed. The tribes became more interested in material wealth and political compatability than obedience to the law. Through intermarriage and religious syncretism, the strength of Israel began to decline. Tribes became independent and many sanctuaries were built in addition to the one at Shiloh. Rather than progression and victory, the Book of Judges portrays the sad story of retrogression and failure.

The Book of Judges serves as both a challenge and a warning. It is a challenge because it illustrates the fact that God can and will work in behalf of men when they turn to Him. It is a warning to all, that God will not tolerate sin.

The books of Joshua and Judges are also books of action. They involve conquest and conflict. In the light of the situations, the admonition given to Joshua on the eve of march is significant and with important application today: "This book of the Law shall not depart out of thy mouth; thou shalt meditate therein day and night, that thou mayest observe to do all that is written therein: for then thou shalt make thy way prosperous and then thou shalt have good success" (Josh. 1:8).

RUTH

Chapter 12

SOJOURN IN MOAB
(Ruth 1–2)

Treasures are many times discovered in the most unlikely places. Once while walking across the dry, barren hills of Judah, I looked down amidst the stones and saw a small coin. This discovery changed my view of that immediate area. Whereas I had considered the area as never having been occupied and therefore of little importance, it now took on a new character.

The Book of Ruth is, in some respects, like that coin. Out of the gloom and decadence of the period of the Judges comes this refreshing, wholesome love story which is an excellent illustration of the grace of God at work in the Old Testament era. The period of the judges was marked by sensuousness and shallow passions. Remember the attitudes and acts of Samson which failed to rise above the trends of his day. In striking contrast to this is the story of Ruth, the Moabitess. Her story is one of godly faithfulness and true love. It is the story of sacrifice rather than self-centered interests.

I. INTRODUCTION

A. *The Title of the Book*

This book derives its title from the principal character of the book, Ruth, the Moabitess. It constitutes one of two books in the Old Testament which was named after a woman — Esther being the other. The derivation and meaning of the name Ruth are uncertain. It is felt by some that it is related to the Hebrew verb *rāʿāh* which has the idea of "associating with someone." Others are inclined to regard it as a contraction of the Hebrew word *reʿut* which means "friendship."[48] In both cases the central idea would be "friendship" or "friend." In the English Bible the book constitutes an appropriate appendix to the Book of Judges and serves as an introduction to historical books of Samuel.

---

[48]C. F. Keil and F. Delitzsch, *op. cit.*, p. 466.

B. *Authorship of the Book*

The author of the book is unkown. The historical setting of the book is the time of the Judges (1:1). Since David's name is mentioned in the book (4:22), but not Solomon's, it is probable that it was written during the reign of David. Some have suggested that Samuel may have been the author, but this cannot be verified. Critics generally date the book in the post-exilic period. They suggest that it was written in the time of Ezra and Nehemiah as a protest against their stringent laws prohibiting marriage between Jews and non-Jews. Several Aramaisms are cited as further proof of its late composition. However, these arguments are not conclusive and rest on questionable presuppositions. The fact that King David is mentioned and not Solomon seems to be an argument in favor of a rather early date of composition. A later writer would surely have made some mention of Solomon in this book.

C. *Position in the Canon*

In the Hebrew Bible this book is listed with the *ketubîm*, the third division, it appears fifth though, according to the Talmud, it must have been first at one time in that division. It is one of five books included in the *megilloth*. The *megilloth* consisted of five books which were read in the synagogue on five special occasions or festivals during the year. In printed editions of the Hebrew Old Testament these books are usually arranged as follows: Canticles, Ruth, Lamentations, Ecclesiastes and Esther. Ruth is placed in the second position because it was read at the feast of weeks, later known as Pentecost, the second of five special festivals. Greek translators of the Old Testament Scriptures considered the book an appendix to the Book of Judges and therefore gave it no special title of its own. Later editions of the Septuagint, however, inserted the expression *telos ton kriton* ("the end of the judges") to indicate the break between Judges and Ruth.

D. *Purposes of the Book*

Some see only one purpose in the book, which is "to provide a genealogical link between Judah and David." However, a careful study of the book from all perspectives indicates that there are at least four purposes for the writing of this book: (1) To exhibit faith and godliness in the time of apostasy. (2) To illustrate a concept of a kinsman redeemer. (3) To show that the scope of God's grace in the Old Testament included the Gentiles. (4) To trace the ancestry of David back to Judah. This latter point is recognized by most all writers. For example, Keil and Delitzsch make the following observation:

> In this conclusion the meaning and tendency of the whole narrative is brought clearly to light. The genealogical proof of the descent of David from Perez through Boaz and the Moabitess Ruth (chap. 4:18-22) forms not only the end, but the starting point, of the history contained in the book.[49]

The data supplied by the Book of Ruth are essential to the reconstruction of the Messianic line in the Old Testament. The genealogical information in Ruth is employed by both Matthew and Luke (Matt. 1:3-6; Luke 3:32-33). Of special interest in these genealogies is the fact that the names of four women are included. This is unique simply because genealogical lists are usually based on male descendants. Also of interest in this regard is the character of the women named. In addition to Ruth the following women appear in these genealogies connected with the line of Christ: Tamar (Gen. 38), Rahab (Josh. 6), and Bathsheba (II Sam. 11).

E. Historical Background

According to 1:1, the historical context of the Book of Ruth is the days of the Judges. While none of the judges are named in the Book of Ruth, many feel these events fall in the days of Gideon, due to the fact that a famine is mentioned during this period (cf. Judg. 6:3-4).

The early part of the story takes place in the land of Moab. The Bible gives us a rather complete picture of the origin and development of the nation of Moabites. According to Genesis 19:37, Moab was the son of Lot by an incestuous union with his

---

[49]Ibid.

eldest daughter. The development of the nation of Moab from the offspring of Lot is not described in Scripture. It is not until the exodus period that we read about Moabite activity to any great degree. Evidently, the Amorites had taken control of Moabite territory at the time of Israel's movement through their land. Balak, King of Moab, did not attempt to stop Israel militarily. He employed the services of Balaam, from Mesopotamia. In spite of the enmity that existed between Israel and Moab, God forbade Israel to fight with Moab for possession of that land (Deut. 2:9). The Moabites were later the chief source of Israel's agony. For eighteen years under the leadership of Eglon they oppressed Israel (Judg. 3). The sojourn of Elimelech and his family in the land of Moab probably took place after the defeat of the Moabite peoples. Some years later, King Saul was forced to defeat the Moabites (I Sam. 14:47). It appears that during the early days of David, however, friendly conditions existed, for David was able to leave his parents under Moabite protection (I Sam. 22:3-4). The chief deity of the Moabites was Chemosh (Num. 21:29), who seems to have been propitiated by human sacrifices (see II Kings 3:26-27). The famous Moabite Stone, discovered at Dibon, gives us further information about the conflict between Moab and the dynasty of Omri.

F. *Basic Outline*

1. *The Journey of Ruth* (1:1-22)
2. *The Gleaning of Ruth* (2:1-23)
3. *The Appeal of Ruth* (3:1-18)
4. *The Marriage of Ruth* (4:1-22)

II. THE JOURNEY OF RUTH (1:1-22)

A. *Ten Years of Tragedy* (1:1-5)

As already noted, verse one provides the immediate historical background for the events that follow. The move of Elimelech and his family from Bethlehem to Moab was brought about by a serious famine in the land. Since this event is placed during the time of the judges, it is fair to conclude that this famine was a special judgment of God upon His people (cf. Lev. 26: 14, 16; Deut. 11:16-17). The sojourn of Elimelech and his family is reminiscent of similar events that occurred during the patriarchal period. Abraham (Gen. 12:10), Isaac (Gen. 26:1), and Jacob (Gen. 26:1-4) all sought aid in other lands during similar famines. It is also significant to observe that problems usually attended such migrations on the part of God's people.

The names of the individuals involved in this story are significant in the light of the events that take place. Elimelech literally means "my God is King" and might reflect his faith in Jehovah. Naomi can be translated "my sweetness" or "delight" or "the sweet one." The meaning of the names of the two sons are more difficult to ascertain. Mahlon probably means "weakly" and comes from the Hebrew root *ḥālāh* meaning "to be sick." The name of the other son, Chilion, is more difficult to interpret. It is generally regarded as meaning "wasting" or "pining." After living in Moab for some period of time, Elimelech died, leaving Naomi and her two sons. Following the death of their father, the two boys married Moabite girls whose names are given as Orpah and Ruth (v. 4). The two sons, plus their wives and their mother, remained in the land of Moab about ten years. During this time both the sons died, leaving three widows (v. 5).

The marriage of the two sons to Moabite girls has raised a number of questions. Some scholars feel that the marriage was legitimate since Moab was not specifically mentioned in Deuteronomy 7:3. However, since both Ezra (Ezra 9:1) and Nehemiah (Neh. 13:23) apply this law to the Moabites, it should be regarded as including this nation. It is obvious from the study of Deuteronomy 7 that not every nation is mentioned, only the outstanding political enemies that controlled Canaan at that time. Jewish commentators have generally regarded that the death of the two sons was an evidence of divine judgment for such intermarriage.

B. *The Journey to Bethlehem* (1:6-22)

1. *A Search for Alternatives* (1:6-15)

With her sons and husband dead, Naomi decided to return to Bethlehem where relatives still lived. She had received word

160

CONQUEST AND CRISIS

that the famine had ended and the Lord again was blessing His people (v. 6). This statement in verse 6 indicates that the famine in verse 1 was regarded as a judgment from God. As they began their journey home, Naomi realized that the land of Israel offered little for these girls. She encouraged them to return to their mother's house (v. 8). The expression "mother's house" is somewhat unique. Normally we should expect her to refer to their "father's house." A number of explanations have been offered for this unusual statement. Some have felt that the father of these girls was dead. Another possibility is that Naomi felt the greatest comfort at this time could be found in the presence of their mother. In any event, she encouraged their return and offered a blessing to them. Her reference to their kindness to their husbands indicated that the girls had been responsible wives and had perhaps adopted the faith of their husbands. She indicated that she hoped that they would find rest in the house of their husbands (v. 9). Naomi's use of "rest" here is probably synonymous with the idea of marriage (cf. 3:1). The girls responded that they would return with her to Bethlehem (v. 10). As they continued their journey toward Bethlehem, Naomi again implored them to return to their own people, for she was too old to bear sons and she had no husband (vv. 11-12). She could offer them no hope and, therefore, she felt that their hope at this time lay in Moab.

It is interesting that Naomi reflected upon her experiences from a theological point of view, for she saw the hand of God in her circumstance (v. 13). This observation included both blessing (v. 6) and judgment (vv. 13, 21). When Orpah heard the words of Naomi, she again wept along with Ruth, but this time she returned to her people and to her gods (v. 15). When Naomi challenged Ruth to do the same, it was clear that Naomi's test was not only a practical and emotional one, but a theological one as well. The only hope for these Moabite girls in Israel would be that they should completely forsake their people and their gods. According to Mosaic Law an Ammonite and a Moabite were not to enter the congregation of Israel (Deut. 23:3). If the faith of Ruth were really genuine, she would not be tempted to return to the gods of Moab.

2. A Daring Decision (1:16-18)

The response of Ruth to Naomi, recorded in verses 16, 17 contains some of the most beautiful language in all the Old Testament. It is one of the highest expressions of faith to be found in the Bible. The words of Ruth are a good example of what Christ had in mind when He uttered the words recorded in Matthew 19:27-30. Ruth concluded her testimony and her commitment of faith with the well-known oath, "The Lord do so to me and more also if ought but death part thee and me" (v. 17). In effect, she invoked the punishment of God if she should let anything less than death part her from Naomi. The same formula appears in I Samuel 3:17 where Eli invoked God's punishment against Samuel if he should hide from him anything that God had revealed to him. It also appears in I Samuel 25:22 where David used the formula as an oath that he would destroy Nabal and all those belonging to his household. David once again used the formula in his oath to make Amasa captain of the armies (II Sam. 19:13). When Naomi saw that the faith of Ruth was unshakable and unchangeable, she encouraged Ruth to continue with her to Bethlehem. The journey they made was not an easy one. It would have covered approximately seventy-five miles, assuming they were abiding in the Moabite tableland. The descent from the mountains of Moab to the Jordan Valley would have been 4,500 feet, and the journey would have also required an ascent to Bethlehem of 3,750 feet through the hills of Judah.

3. Theological Perspectives (1:19-22)

As they entered the city, they were undoubtedly greeted by some of the women of the town, for the verb used in verse 19 is a feminine plural (Heb. to'marnāh). The question they asked was, "Is this Naomi?" Naomi's response to them is interesting. She said, "Call me not Naomi [which means 'sweetness'], call me Mara [which means 'bitterness']." Naomi recognized that she had gone out full and rich, while she had returned empty and poor. She again recognized the hand of God in the history of her life and this time she made reference to šaday. This name of God is associated with His power and His might. Such expressions on the lips of a believer are significant, for they recognize that all things work together for good to all those who are called according to the purpose of God (cf. Rom. 8:28). It was probably very difficult for Naomi to face many of her friends, but her frank testimory is a credit to her godly character. According to verse 22, they returned at the beginning of the barley harvest, thus placing the event in the month of April.

III. THE GLEANING OF RUTH (2:1-23)

A. *Ruth Meets Boaz* (2:1-18)

Boaz, according to verse 1, was a "friend" or "acquaintance" (Heb. *moyda'*) of Naomi's husband. He was also described as a "mighty man of valor" (Heb. *gibor ḥayil*), here better translated a "man of wealth" or a "man of property." Ruth then requested that she be permitted to go to the fields to glean grain after the reapers. Ruth evidently had knowledge of the law of Moses which indicated that those owning fields were to permit gleaners to gather grain after the reapers. This was done in order that the poor might have adequate provision made for their needs (cf. Lev. 19:9; 23:22; Deut. 24:19). The fact that Naomi did not join in the gleaning probably indicates that she was either weary from the journey or incapable of such activity because of age. Not all farmers would have permitted the poor to do this in their fields, and this is why Ruth said that she would search after the one "in whose sight I shall find grace" (v. 2). The very fact that Boaz permitted her in the fields was an indication of his godly character. As Ruth prepared to enter the fields, we are told, "chance her chanced" or "it happened" that she came on the part of the field belonging to Boaz (v. 3). What was chance from a human point of view was a perfect plan from a divine point of view. Boaz again gave evidence of his godly character as he walked through the fields. The relationship between himself and the reapers was an ideal one. His greeting was, "The Lord be with you"; and they answered him, "The Lord bless you" (v. 4). If the laborer-management situation were conditioned by such theology, perhaps many of the problems would be solved in a shorter period of time. In any event, as Boaz

Reaping in the Fields East of Bethlehem (cf. Ruth 2:4). Matson Photo Service

went through the fields, Ruth caught his eye. He asked, "Whose damsel is this?" (Heb. *na'arāh*, v. 5). Those in the field identified her as the young lady who had returned with Naomi from the land of Moab (v. 6). Ruth was a good worker. According to verse 7, she spent very little time resting. Boaz was probably impressed with her faithfulness and her love for her mother-in-law. He went out of his way to show kindness and love toward her (cf. vv. 12-16). At the end of the day she had gathered approximately thirty pounds of barley (v. 17). After this, she returned to her mother-in-law and reported the events of the day.

B. *Ruth Reports to Naomi* (2:19-23)

The meeting that evening must have been an interesting one. Naomi, very anxious to hear of the events of the day, inquired of Ruth as to where she worked and how she fared. When the name of Boaz was mentioned, she immediately praised the Lord (vv. 19-20). Naomi identified Boaz as a *go'ēl;* that is, a near kinsman or a kinsman redeemer. Ruth evidently had freedom to glean all during the barley harvest. They had returned from Moab at the beginning of the barley harvest (1:22) and Ruth continued to glean until the end of the barley harvest (2:23). During that time the faithfulness and the love of Ruth probably impressed Boaz all the more.

The story of Ruth through the first two chapters is a thrilling one. It is one of simplicity and tragedy, but out of this tragedy the Lord began to work, and His sovereign power was displayed and His will accomplished. Far too often believers surrender to situations of life simply because of loss or death, when, in effect, they have not given God the full opportunity to exercise His power and to display His glory. Again we are reminded by the apostle Paul that "all things work together for good to them that love God, to them who are the called according to his purpose."

Chapter 13

RUTH AND BOAZ
(Ruth 3–4)

When Naomi discovered the acquaintance that Ruth had made with Boaz, she immediately took steps to encourage this relationship. Naomi was faced with two critical problems. First, how should the name of Elimelech be maintained among the tribes of Israel, when he and his sons were dead? Secondly, what steps should be taken to protect the inheritance, which Elimelech had evidently left in Naomi's trust? The marriage of Ruth and Boaz could care for both of these problems. Chapter 3 describes the arrangement and procedures adopted by Naomi and Ruth in an attempt to solve the problems.

I. THE APPEAL OF RUTH (3:1-18)

A. *Naomi's Plan* (3:1-6)

When Naomi recognized Boaz as a near kinsman and realized that he had a special interest in Ruth, she immediately took steps to encourage the marriage of these two. Ruth 3:1 reflects that interest, for she made mention of the fact that she should seek "rest" for Ruth. The use of the word "rest" here has reference to marriage and a home (cf. 1:9). Ruth was instructed to go to the threshing floor in the evening (v. 2). The early evening was one of the best times for winnowing because of the breezes which would come up from the Mediterranean coast. It is also possible that this was a time of danger and therefore necessary for owners to remain with the grain at the threshing floors. Ruth was instructed to make note of the place where he should rest that evening. She was to go there and "uncover his feet" and lie down with him (v. 4). In the eyes of many observers, this represents an immoral act. However, when the customs of Israel are taken into view, rather than a scene of immorality, we have one of legal appeal. Verse 6 informs us that Ruth obeyed her mother-in-law, which again appears to be an evidence of the faith and obedience of Ruth.

B. *Ruth's Performance* (3:7-18)

1. *The Morality of the Act* (v. 7)

The question which naturally arises at this point regards the
condition or the state of Boaz on this occasion. Verse 7 has
led some interpreters to feel that Boaz was drunk at this time,
for the text describes him as having eaten "and drunk and his
heart was merry." It is true that on occasion "to make the
heart merry" can refer to the excessive use of wine and therefore drunkenness. However, this is not necessarily always the
case. Many times the expression "merry" or "happy heart" merely
refers to satisfaction after good eating (cf. I Kings 21:7; Judg.
19:6-9). Most probably, the word "merry" suggests that Boaz
was happy and had a sense of well-being since, following the
years of famine (1:1), he now had an abundant harvest.[50]
One Targum interprets this expression by the following reading:
"He (Boaz) blessed the name of Jehovah."[51]

The morality of this situation has also been questioned by
virtue of the fact that Ruth "uncovered his feet" and laid down
with him (v. 7). Verse 9 records the request of Ruth for Boaz
to cover her with his "skirt" (Heb. *kānāp* cf. 2:12). In its full-
est historical and cultural context, the events described in these
verses take on a note of ethical and moral beauty. According
to Hebrew law, Ruth "was entitled to call upon her nearest of
kin to fulfill the various duties of a responsible kinsman."[52]
Ruth's actions were, therefore, in accord with previous revelation and well-known customs. Pfeiffer remarks, "The custom of
a man's placing a corner of his garment over a maiden as a
token of marriage is known among the Arabs."[53] The situation
described in Ruth 3 perhaps parallels this modern Arabic custom. Ruth probably laid crosswise at the feet of Boaz and
covered herself with the corners of his garment, thus requesting
Boaz to become the kinsman redeemer (cf. v. 9). Boaz fully

[50]Francis D. Nichol (ed.), *Seventh-day Adventist Commentary*, Vol. II
(Washington D. C., Review and Herald Publishing Assoc., 1954), p. 438.
[51]James Morrison, *Ruth, The Pulpit Commentary* Joseph S. Exell and
H. D. M. Spence (eds.), Vol. 8 (Grand Rapids: Wm. B. Eerdmans Publishing Co., 1950), p. 48.
[52]*Ibid.*
[53]Charles Pfeiffer, *op. cit.*, p. 271.

understood the request as evidenced in verses 10 through 12. It is interesting to observe that in verse 11 the moral character of Ruth was reaffirmed by Boaz in the expression "Thou art a virtuous woman" (Heb. *'ēšeṯ ḥayil 'āt*). This description of Ruth, along with the expressions applied to her in Chapter 2, vindicates her moral character and behavior. There was an obvious concern on the part of Boaz to maintain that pure image before the village (vv. 11-13).

2. *The Legality of the Situation* (vv. 12-18)

Boaz, having received the request of Ruth, pointed out that he was not legally able to assume kinsman responsibilities at this stage, for there was a kinsman nearer than himself. Boaz was only a nephew of Elimelech, whereas a brother was probably still living. According to Hebrew law, the brother of Elimelech bore first responsibility as kinsman redeemer (Heb. *gō'ēl*). Ruth remained at his feet until morning and rose up "before one could know another" (v. 14). The verb translated "know" in this text is not the one which has reference to sexual intercourse, but another verb having the idea "to discern or recognize" (Heb. *yakîr*). Before leaving the threshing floor, Boaz gave her six measures of barley to take back to Naomi (v. 15). When she came to the home of her mother-in-law, she was asked, "Who art thou, my daughter?" (v. 16). The question of Naomi can be interpreted two ways. It might mean it was so dark that she could only recognize her visitor as a woman and therefore asked for further identification. Or, perhaps the question has the idea of "How did you fare, my daughter?" (RSV). The last command of Boaz is recorded in verse 18. Ruth was requested to remain at home (sit still) until the legal problems of the matter had been cared for.

II. THE MARRIAGE OF RUTH (4:1-22)

A. *The Legal Process* (4:1-13)

In order to clear up the legal complications that hindered the marriage, Boaz organized a hearing at the gate of the city (v. 1). The area inside the gates was commonly used as a place of legal transaction in Hebrew cities (cf. Deut. 21:19-21). The

nearer kinsman was informed of the hearing, and ten elders of
the city of Bethlehem were selected to hear the case (v. 2).
Evidently ten was the necessary quorum for this type of case.
The problems of the case at hand were immediately brought
before the ten elders and the nearest kinsman. The first problem dealt with by Boaz involved the inheritance of Elimelech;
namely, a parcel of land. Naomi was about to sell this land
(v. 3). The verb which occurs in verse three — "selleth" — is a
perfect form, normally translated as a past ("sold"; Heb.
mākerāh). However, it is better translated "about to sell" here
because of the information supplied in verses 5 and 9 (". . .
of the hand of Naomi"), indicating that she had not yet
disposed of the land. Evidently, Naomi intended to sell
the rights for use of the land until the time of Jubilee. The
responsibility of nearest of kinsman was to purchase that property in order that it should not fall into the hands of strangers,
but remain in the family of Elimelech (v. 4). Redemption of
the deceased brother's property was one of three responsibilities
ascribed to the go'ēl in the Old Testament (Lev. 25:25). The
other two involved the avenging of the blood of a deceased
brother (Deut. 19:22) and levirate marriage (Deut. 25:5).

The offer of Boaz was attractive at first to the nearest of kinsman, for if he could bring this parcel of land under his control,
even though it might cost him a high price, the productivity of
the land would more than pay him for his effort. However,
Boaz did not leave the issue at that point. He further stated
that if the nearest kinsman were going to be a go'ēl and resume
the responsibility of land redemption, then he was also responsible to raise up a name for the deceased brother; namely, to
fulfill the requirement of levirate marriage (v. 5). Boaz, at
this point, used some legal skill, for strictly speaking, the kinsman redeemer was not responsible to fulfill every legal obligation of the go'ēl. Boaz, however, connected the two and made
one contingent upon the other. As the nearer kinsman contem-
plated this situation, the offer of the purchase of land became
less attractive.

> He must have reasoned that in order to buy Naomi's land he
> would have to invest a part of the value of his own estate, or
> inheritance. Then should he father a child of Ruth's that son

would in Mahlon's name, not his own, become the heir of land which he bought with money from his own estate. He seemed willing to redeem Naomi's property if it should not hurt him financially, or if he might possibly gain by it, but he could not accept the responsibility if it should eventuate in a diminution of his own resources and a consequent injustice to his own heirs.[54]

With this official refusal, Boaz was free both to redeem the property and to marry Ruth. The transfer of kinsman responsibility was symbolized by the nearest of kinsman removing his sandal and giving it to Boaz. This custom is well known, not only from the Book of Ruth, but also from Deuteronomy 25:9. It has been further attested in the Nuzi Documents.[55] This marriage had its first goal to raise up the name of the deceased upon his inheritance (v. 10). In this sense, the marriage of Boaz to Ruth was similar to a levirate marriage, but due to the fact that Boaz was not a near kinsman to Elimelech, it differs from levirate marriage which is described in the Mosaic Law.[56]

B. *The Divine Blessing* (4:14-22)

The marriage of Ruth and Boaz was blessed by the Lord in the birth of a son (v. 13). It is interesting that the women of the town of Bethlehem praised Naomi for this event, for the name of her husband would not be blotted out in the land of Israel (v. 14). The great affection of Naomi for the child is evidenced by the fact that she nursed it when it was quite young (v. 16). Notice also that the women of the village described the son as that which was born to Naomi (v. 17), and they gave him the name Obed which simply means "servant."

---

[54]S. Herbert Bess, *Systems of Land Tenure in Ancient Israel* (Unpublished Ph.D. dissertation, University of Michigan, 1963), p. 78.

[55]See E. A. Speiser, "Of Shoes and Shekels," *Bulletin of the American Schools of Oriental Research* No. 77 (Feb., 1940), p. 17.

Ernest R. Lacheman, "Notes on Ruth 4:7-8," *Journal of Biblical Literature* LXI (1937), pp. 53-56.

[56]For an excellent discussion of the legal aspects of this marriage see H. H. Rowley, *The Servant of the Lord* (Oxford: Basil Blackwell, second edition, revised, 1965) pp. 171 ff.

The Book of Ruth concludes with the genealogy from Pharez to King David (vv. 18-22). The chart below will help to illustrate this important line.

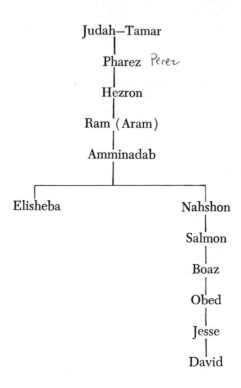

It is very fitting that our story of the Judges period should end on this note. The story of Ruth is one of tragedy and triumph. What seemed like a hopeless situation turned out to be one in which the Lord was fully glorified and His purposes accomplished. The love of Boaz and Ruth along with their sensitiveness to the laws of Israel are refreshing in a time when those about them had abandoned the truth of Scripture. Among the rugged, dry, barrenness of the Judges period, the Book of Ruth is indeed a precious gem to behold.

BIBLIOGRAPHY

Adams, J. McKee. *Biblical Backgrounds*. Nashville: Broadman Press, 1934.

Aharoni, Yohanan. *The Land of the Bible*. Trans. A. F. Rainey. Philadelphia: The Westminster Press, 1962.

Aharoni, Yohanan and Avi-yonah, Michael. *The Macmillan Bible Atlas*. New York: The Macmillan Co., 1968.

Albright, William F. *The Biblical Period*. Pittsburgh: Harper and Row, 1955.

_____. *The Archaeology of Palestine*. Baltimore: Penguin Books, 1961.

_____. *Archaeology and the Religion of Israel*. Baltimore: The Johns Hopkins Press, 1953.

Archer, Gleason L. *A Survey of Old Testament Introduction*. Chicago: Moody Press, 1964.

Baly, Denis. *The Geography of the Bible*. New York: Harper & Bros., 1957.

Bettan, Israel. *The Five Scrolls*. Cincinnati: Union of American Hebrew Congregations, 1950.

Bright, John. *A History of Israel*. Philadelphia: Westminster Press, 1959.

Brown, Francis; Driver, S. R.; Briggs, Charles A. *A Hebrew and English Lexicon of the Old Testament*. Oxford: The Clarendon Press, 1952.

Burney, C. F. *The Book of Judges*. 2nd ed. London: Rivingtons, 1930.

Crosby, Howard. *Expository Notes on the Book of Joshua*. New York: Robert Carter and Bros., 1875.

Davidson, Francis; Stibbs, A. M. & Kevan, E. F. (eds.) *New Bible Commentary*. Grand Rapids: Wm. B. Eerdmans Publishing Co.. 1953.

Davis, John D. *A Dictionary of the Bible*. Grand Rapids: Baker Book House, 1954.

DeHaan, M. R. *The Romance of Redemption*. Grand Rapids: Zondervan Publishing House, 1958.

Douglas, George C. M. *The Book of Judges*. Edinburgh: T & T Clark, 1881.

Douglas, J. D. (ed). *The New Bible Dictionary*. Grand Rapids: Wm. B. Eerdmans Publishing Co., 1962.

Driver, G. R. *Canaanite Myths and Legends*. Edinburgh: T & T Clark, 1956.

Exell, Joseph S. and Spence, H. D. M. (eds.). *The Pulpit Commentary.* Vol. 4. Grand Rapids: Wm. B. Eerdmans Publishing Co., 1950.

Fay, F. R. *Joshua, Commentary on the Holy Scriptures.* Trans. by Philip Schaff. Grand Rapids: Zondervan Publishing House, 1915.
Freiderberg, S. *Joshua, An Annotated Hebrew Text.* London: William Heinemann, 1913.

Garstang, John. *Joshua-Judges: The Foundation of Bible History.* New York: Richard R. Smith, Inc., 1931.
Garstang, John and Garstang, J. B. E. *The Story of Jericho.* London: Marshall, Morgan & Scott, Ltd., New Edition, Revised. 1948.

Heinisch, Paul. *Theology of the Old Testament.* The Liturgical Press, 1955.

Ironside, H. A. *Addresses on the Book of Joshua.* New York: Loizeaux Bros., 1950.

Jamieson, Robert; Fausset, A. R.; Brown, David. *Commentary on the Whole Bible.* Grand Rapids: Zondervan Publishing House, n.d.

Kaufman, Yehezkel. *The Biblical Account of the Conquest of Palestine.* Jerusalem: Hebrew University Magnes Press, 1935.
Keil, C. F. and Delitzsch, F. *Biblical Commentary on the Old Testament: Joshua, Judges, Ruth.* Grand Rapids: Wm. B. Eerdmans Publishing Co., 1950.
Kenyon, Kathleen. *Archaeology in the Holy Land.* New York: Frederick A. Praeger, 1960.
----------. *Digging Up Jericho.* London: Ernest Benn Limited, 1957.
Kitchen, K. A. *Ancient Orient and Old Testament.* Chicago: Inter-Varsity Press, 1966.

Lloyd, John. *The Book of Joshua.* London: Hodder and Stoughton, 1886.

Mauro, Philip. *Ruth: The Satisfied Stranger.* Swengel, Pa.: Bible Truth Depot, 1963.
McGee, J. Vernon. *Ruth, The Romance of Redemption.* Findlay, Ohio: The Dunham Publishing Co., 1962.
McKenzie, John L. *The World of the Judges.* Englewood Cliffs, N. J.: Prentice-Hall, Inc., 1966.
Mendenhall, George E. *Law and Covenant in Israel and the Ancient Near East.* Pittsburgh: The Biblical Colloquium, 1955.

Morrison, James. *The Pulpit Commentary*, Vol. 4. Grand Rapids: Wm. B. Eerdmans Publishing Co., 1950.

Nichol, Francis D. (ed.). *Seventh-day Adventist Commentary*. Vol. 2. Washington, D.C.: Review and Herald Publishing Assoc., 1954.

Payne, J. Barton. *The Theology of the Older Testament*. Grand Rapids: Zondervan Publishing House, 1962.
Pfeiffer, Charles F. and Harrison, Everett F. (eds.). *The Wycliffe Bible Commentary*. Chicago: Moody Press, 1963.
Pink, Arthur W. *Gleanings in Joshua*. Chicago: Moody Press, 1964.
Pritchard, James B. (ed.). *Ancient Near Eastern Texts Relating to the Old Testament*. Princeton: Princeton University Press, 1955.

Ridout, Samuel. *Lectures on the Books of Judges and Ruth*. New York: Loizeaux Brothers, Inc., 1958.
Rowley, H. H. *The Rediscovery of the Old Testament*. Philadelphia: The Westminster Press, 1946.
--------------. *The Servant of the Lord*. Oxford: Basil Blackwell, 2nd Edition Revised, 1965.

Simons, J. *The Geographical and Topographical Texts of the Old Testament*. Leiden: E. J. Brill, 1959.
Simpson, C. A. *Composition of the Book of Judges*. Oxford: Blackwell, 1957.
Slotki, J. R. *The Five Megilloth*. Abraham Cohen (ed.) London: The Soncino Press, 1952.
Smith, Louise P. "The Book of Ruth" *The Interpreter's Bible*. Vol. 2. New York: Abingdon Press, 1953.

Totten, Charles A. *Joshua's Long Day and the Dial of Ahaz*. Haverhill, Mass.: Destiny Publishers, 1941.

Unger, Merrill F. *Archaeology and the Old Testament*. Grand Rapids: Zondervan Publishing House, 1954.
--------------. (ed.). *Unger's Bible Dictionary*. Chicago: Moody Press, 1957.

Velikovsky, Immanuel. *Worlds in Collision*. New York: Macmillan, 1950.

Watson, Robert A. *Judges and Ruth, The Expositor's Bible*. New York: A. C. Armstrong and Sons, 1899.
Williams, George. *The Student's Commentary on the Holy Scriptures*. London: Oliphants Ltd., 1949.

ARTICLES AND PERIODICALS

Anderson, Bernhard W. "The Place of Shechem in the Bible" *The Biblical Archaeologist*. XX. (Feb., 1957, No. 1.)

Davis, John J. "The Patriarchs Knowledge of Jehovah" *Grace Journal*. Winona Lake: Grace Theological Seminary, 1963. Vol. 4, No. 1.

Lacheman, Ernest. "Notes on Ruth 4:7-8" *Journal of Biblical Literature*. LXI, 1937.

Ralph Marcus. "The Word Sibboleth Again" *Bulletin of the American Schools of Oriental Research*. No. 87, Oct. 1942.

Rea, John. "The Time of the Oppression and the Exodus" *Grace Journal*. Winona Lake: Grace Theological Seminary, 1961. Vol. 2, No. 1.

--------------. "New Light on the Wilderness Journey and the Conquest" *Grace Journal*. Winona Lake: Grace Theological Seminary, 1962. Vol. 2, No. 2.

Speiser, E. A. "Of Shoes and Shekels" *Bulletin of the American Schools of Oriental Research*. No. 77 (Feb., 1940).

--------------. "The Shibboleth Incident (Judges 12:6)" *Bulletin of the American Schools of Oriental Research*. No. 85 (Feb., 1942).

Wilson, Robert Dick. "What Does 'The Sun Stood Still' Mean?" *Princeton Theological Review* XVI (1918) pp. 46-47.

INDEX

175

176   CONQUEST AND CRISIS